THE LIVING WORD COMMENTARY

Editor
Everett Ferguson

The
Acts of the Apostles
Part II
13:1–28:31

The
Acts of the Apostles
Part II
13:1–28:31

Richard Oster

SWEET PUBLISHING COMPANY

Austin, Texas

LIBRARY OF CONGRESS CATALOG CARD NUMBER 79-63269

ISBN 0-8344-0099-5

PRINTED IN U.S.A.

Acknowledgments

This commentary is based on the text of the Revised Standard Version of the Bible, copyrighted 1946, 1952, 1971, and 1973 by the Division of Christian Education, National Council of Churches, and used by permission.

Quotations from the following works are cited by permission of the publishers: Ernst Haenchen, *Acts of the Apostles*. Philadelphia: Westminster Press, 1971; F. F. Bruce, *Acts of the Apostles*. Grand Rapids: Wm. B. Eerdmans, 1970; John Calvin, *Acts of the Apostles*. Grand Rapids: Wm. B. Eerdmans, 1949; William M. Ramsay, *St. Paul the Traveller and Roman Citizen*. Grand Rapids: Baker Book House, 1951.

Writers in *The Living Word Commentary* series have been given freedom to develop their own understanding of the biblical text. As long as a fair statement is given to alternative interpretations, each writer has been permitted to state his own conclusions. Beyond the general editorial policies, the editors have sought no artificial uniformity, and differences are allowed free expression. A writer is responsible for his contribution alone, and the views expressed are not necessarily the views of the editors or publisher.

5 4 3 2

Contents

IV

Paul's Missionary Tours
13:1–21:25

PAUL'S FIRST JOURNEY, 13:1–14:28

The Antioch Church, 13:1-3

[1] It was just and appropriate that the interracial church at **Antioch** should have been the congregation to bring Paul out of his limited ministry at Tarsus (11:25, 26) and plant him in the midst of far-reaching missionary work among the Jews and Greeks throughout the Roman world. After all, the congregation at Antioch itself was the product of a more liberal form of Jewish Christianity whose missionary attitudes were much less provincial than those of the Jewish Christians whose doctrine was narrowly rooted in Jerusalem (11:19-23; cf. 15:1-5; Gal. 2:11ff.). This more cosmopolitan orientation and racial attitude is significantly reflected in the list of **prophets** (*prophētai*) and **teachers** (*didaskaloi*, only here in Acts) in the Antioch congregation. **Saul** (designated only here as prophet but elsewhere as teacher, 2 Tim. 1:11; cf. 1 Cor. 12:28f.; Eph. 4:11), **Barnabas**, and **Lucius** were diaspora Jews; in fact, the latter two were products of the same Jewish matrix, Cyprus and **Cyrene**, which shaped the Christians who founded the church at

¹**Now in the church at Antioch there were prophets and teachers, Barnabas, Simeon who was called Niger, Lucius of Cyrene, Manaen a member of the court of Herod the tetrarch, and Saul.** ²**While they were worshiping the Lord and fasting, the Holy Spirit said, "Set apart for me Barnabas and Saul for the work to which I have called them."** ³**Then after fasting and praying they laid their hands on them and sent them off.**

Antioch (11:20; cf. Nicolaus proselyte of Antioch in 6:5). Moreover, the very fact that a certain Antiochene Christian leader named **Manaen** could be an intimate friend (*suntrophos*) of the greatly Hellenized Jewish ruler **Herod** Antipas (who built the Gentile city of Tiberias in A.D. 22) testifies both to the penetration of the gospel into the more urbane and aristocratic circles of Antiochene society and to the more open and cosmopolitan perspectives of the church leaders there.

[2] Luke mentions that both **Barnabas and Saul** were **called** and **set apart** and that the recognition of this ordination by the congregation in the laying on of hands was a crucial part of the commissioning. The bringing together of the terms **called** and **set apart** is reminiscent of Paul's way of describing his apostolic consciousness (Rom. 1:1; 1 Cor. 1:1; Gal. 1:15). Being called by the **Spirit** and set apart by human agents constitutes a type of two-pronged confirmation which occurs at other crucial junctures in the New Testament: Jesus' baptism (Luke 3:21f.), Paul's Damascus road revelation (Acts 9:3-19), and Peter's vision of the new missionary direction to Gentiles (Acts 10:1-48) are all examples of this divine intervention accomplished through human agency (cf. 2 Tim. 1:6; 1 Tim. 5:22).

[3] Congregational prayer and fasting were clearly part of early church piety. The evidence, admittedly scanty, would support the suggestion that it was a regular practice in conjunction with the appointment of elders, at least in Paul's churches (14:23; see note on 1:14 on prayer).

⁴So, being sent out by the Holy Spirit, they went down to Seleucia; and from there they sailed to Cyprus. ⁵ When they arrived at Salamis, they proclaimed the word of God in the synagogues of the Jews. And they had John to assist them. ⁶ When they had gone through the whole island as far as Paphos, they came upon a certain magician, a Jewish false prophet, named Bar-Jesus. ⁷ He was with the proconsul, Sergius Paulus, a man of intelligence, who summoned Barnabas and Saul and sought to hear the word of God. ⁸ But Elymas the magician (for that is the meaning of his name) withstood them, seeking to turn away the proconsul from the faith.

Paul and Barnabas on Cyprus, 13:4-12

[4, 5] Leaving **Seleucia**, the port city of Antioch, the two missionaries, with Mark as an assistant (*hupēretēs*), traveled the short distance to **Salamis**, a metropolitan port on the east side of **Cyprus**. Luke's reference to a plurality of **synagogues** in Salamis is quite understandable. According to several ancient sources Judaism was very widespread in the first century (cf. 15:21). One would, therefore, expect to find more than one synagogue in larger urban areas. Paul's cultural heritage as well as his doctrinal convictions always drove him to begin his evangelistic work in synagogues (cf. 17:1 and note on 13:46).

[6-8] The apostles' crossing of the island led them finally to **Paphos**, the seaport capital of the Roman province and consequently the residence of the imperial **proconsul**, **Sergius Paulus**. **Paphos** was a famous site among pagans. The future Roman Emperor Titus visited this location as a pilgrim. In Tacitus' account of the visit he reports that the "temple of the Paphian Venus" was "a place of celebrity both among natives and foreigners" (*Histories* 2:2).

The ensuing narrative of the gospel's advent in Paphos and its struggle against **Elymas the magician** best comes alive when viewed in the religious matrix of ancient Jewish

⁹But Saul, who is also called Paul, filled with the Holy Spirit, looked intently at him ¹⁰and said, "You son of the devil, you enemy of all righteousness, full of all deceit and villainy, will you not stop making crooked the straight paths of the Lord? ¹¹And now, behold, the hand of the Lord is upon you, and you shall be blind and unable to see the sun for a time." Immediately mist and darkness fell upon him and he went about seeking people to lead him by the hand.

---

magicians. It is imperative to note that in spite of the many Old Testament commandments against magic and sorcery, the Jewish religion in the Graeco-Roman era was replete with both magicians and superstitious attitudes. Jesus (Matt. 12:27; Luke 11:19), Luke (Acts 19:13), Josephus (*Antiquities* VIII.ii.5), several church fathers (Justin Martyr, Irenaeus, Origen), as well as ancient secular writers such as Pliny the Elder (*Natural History* 31.18.24), Juvenal (*Satires* 6.545ff.), and Lucian (*Tragodopodagra* 1173), bear testimony to the presence of Jewish exorcists, users of incantations, and workers of magic. Other Greek and Latin authors comment on the singular importance of Jewish books, the name Yahweh, and the person of Moses in the development of ancient magic at large.

It is not surprising, therefore, that the apostles would both encounter and combat such mountebanks in the course of their missionary journeys in the Graeco-Roman world. The only response of Paul is to demonstrate the true power of God against such counterfeit attempts of the devil. We do not know the exact reason that the proconsul **sought to hear the word of God** beyond the fact that he was a man of intelligence (*sunetos*). **Elymas** feared **the faith** and therefore strove to dissuade the proconsul from engaging Paul and his comrades.

[9-11] Paul tersely denounced this false prophet for attempting to arrest the spreading of the kingdom (cf. 1 Thess. 2:16). Luke portrays this as a battle between a

¹²**Then the proconsul believed, when he saw what had occurred, for he was astonished at the teaching of the Lord.**

---

man **filled with the Holy Spirit** and a man born of **the devil**. This same motif of Holy Spirit versus devil was employed by Luke earlier (10:38; see note on Acts 1:5; 5:4f.). By the **hand of the Lord** (not Paul's), this perverter of **righteousness** and sobriety was punished (cf. 8:21) with a blindness so great that even the brilliance of the **sun** was blocked.

[12] There are several important things to observe about the response of the **proconsul**. First of all, he **believed**. Commentators have discussed whether he became a Christian since no baptism is mentioned. We demand too much of Luke if we expect him to mention baptism every time it took place. Second, the occasion for the proconsul's faith was his seeing this miracle, a punitive one in this instance (cf. 8:6; 14:11; 19:11-20; 28:6; Rom. 15:18; 2 Cor. 12:12 for the use of signs and wonders in evangelism; see introduction to ch. 3, part 1, and note on 2:19). Most important, though, the object of the proconsul's astonishment was the **teaching of the Lord**. Luke's expression **astonished at the teaching** (*ekplēssomai epi tē didachē*) is employed in the Gospels to describe people's reaction to the revolutionary teachings of Jesus (Matt. 7:28; 22:33; Mark 1:22; 11:18; Luke 4:32; cf. Matt. 13:54; 19:25; Mark 6:2). Unlike many pagan wonderworkers and specious Christian miracle workers (e.g., Simon Magus) Luke placed the emphasis correctly upon the preaching and teaching facet of Christian miracles. Sir William Mitchell Ramsay correctly perceived the place of this story in Luke's writing:

Bar-Jesus represented the strongest influence on the human will that existed in the Roman world, an influence which must destroy or be destroyed by Christianity, if the latter tried to conquer the Empire. And we cannot wonder that to Luke, familiar with the terrible power of that religion, the Magian seemed the

¹³Now Paul and his company set sail from Paphos, and came to Perga in Pamphylia. And John left them and returned to Jerusalem; ¹⁴but they passed on from Perga and came to Antioch of Pisidia. And on the sabbath day they went into the synagogue and sat down. ¹⁵After the reading of the law and the prophets, the rulers of the synagogue sent to them, saying, "Brethren, if you have any word of exhortation for the people, say it." ¹⁶So Paul stood up, and motioning with his hand said:

---

prominent figure round whom the action moved. (*St. Paul the Traveller and the Roman Citizen*. Grand Rapids: Baker Book House, repr. 1975, p. 79)

Paul and Barnabas at Pisidian Antioch, 13:13-16a

[13] For the first time since leaving Tarsus (11:25), Paul entered Asia Minor. Landing at the port of Attalia, he and Barnabas immediately journeyed the short distance to the Pamphylian city of **Perga**. The extent of Paul's preaching at this site is unknown. Only during his return trip via Perga did Paul speak the word there (14:25). When he refers to his **company**, Luke draws attention to the fact that Paul now took over leadership of the mission. Whereas Barnabas had been mentioned first until now, with very few exceptions it is Paul who is henceforth accorded the place of prominence.

[14] The next city in Paul's journey was **Antioch**. Paul's base of operations there was the local **synagogue**. Pisidian Antioch and other cities which Paul visited in this area (e.g., Derbe, Iconium, Lystra) were part of the Roman Galatia and the recipients of Paul's letter to the churches in Galatia.

[15, 16a] Luke's abbreviated description of the sabbath-day synagogue service rightly includes a mention of **the reading of the law and the prophets** (cf. Luke 4:16ff.) and the existence of officials known as **rulers of the synagogue**, the latter being a regular part of the synagogue organization

"Men of Israel, and you that fear God, listen. [17] The God of this people Israel chose our fathers and made the people great during their stay in the land of Egypt, and with uplifted arm he led them out of it. [18] And for about forty years he bore with[m] them in the wilderness. [19] And when he had destroyed seven nations in the land of Canaan, he gave them their land as an inheritance, for about four hundred and fifty years. [20] And after that he gave them judges until Samuel the prophet.

[m] Other ancient authorities read *cared for* (Deut. 1.31)

(cf. Mark 5:22; Luke 8:41; Acts 18:8, 17). A typical synagogue service in antiquity consisted of the following parts: (1) Recital of the *Shema* (Deut. 6:4-9), (2) Prayer of Eighteen Benedictions, (3) Reading of the Law and Prophets, and (4) Exposition of the Scriptures by a qualified male individual (cf. comments of Philo, *Special Laws* II.15.61-62; in Eusebius' *Preparation of the Gospel* 8.7.12-13). The request for **a word of exhortation** afforded Paul the opportunity to preach from the Old Testament about the Christ. Paul arose and gestured in order to get the attention of his audience and secure its silence (cf. 12:17; 21:40; 26:2).

Sermon at Antioch of Pisidia, 13:16b-41

Israel's History, 13:16b-25. [16b] Luke has already mentioned the power of Paul's preaching (9:20-22), but this provides us with the first extended example. Luke's record of Paul's sermon is evidently abbreviated; we can, nevertheless, trust that it communicates the central points Paul made to his listeners.

[17-20] As in most synagogue sermons to Jews and those that **fear God** (see notes on Acts 10:2 on Godfearers) the apostle began this story of redemptive history with the Lord's election of Israel, thereby inextricably linking the church's message with God's prior deeds of redemptive

²¹ **Then they asked for a king; and God gave them Saul the son of Kish, a man of the tribe of Benjamin, for forty years.** ²² **And when he had removed him, he raised up David to be their king; of whom he testified and said, 'I have found in David the son of Jesse a man after my heart, who will do all my will.'** ²³ **Of this man's posterity God has brought to Israel a Savior, Jesus, as he promised.**

---

history. The exodus from Egypt, wilderness wanderings, apostasy of the people, and the conquest of Palestine form the main features of Paul's brief sketch (cf. Stephen's speech, ch. 7). Israel was able to conquer **seven nations in Canaan** (listed in Deut. 7:1) only because of the Lord's support and guidance to the possession of the inheritance, the land.

The problematic **four hundred and fifty years** can be explained in different ways, and all have been put forth by Bible scholars. The majority view is that the four hundred and fifty years refers to the period of Egyptian sojourning (four hundred years: cf. Acts 7:6), the wilderness wanderings (about forty years), and the time between the entry of Canaan and the distribution of the inheritance (about five years, Joshua 14:6-12). This theory is designed to account for the expression in 13:20 **and after that**, which implies that the four hundred and fifty years totally preceded the period of the judges and the possession of the inheritance. An alternative explanation is that the phrase **for about four hundred and fifty years** should be read parenthetically between **as an inheritance** and **after that**.

[21] Paul continues his argument by referring to God's dealings with Israel through kings. First **Saul**, from the apostle's own **tribe of Benjamin**, and then David were appointed by God as king.

[22, 23] The concept of the Davidic covenant in the Old Testament is rich and splendid in thought and is applied in a variety of ways to Jesus in the New Testament writings (e.g., Matt. 1:1; 9:27; 12:23; 15:22; 20:30, 31; 21:9, 15; Luke

²⁴**Before his coming John had preached a baptism of repentance to all the people of Israel. ²⁵And as John was finishing
his course, he said, 'What do you suppose that I am? I am not
he. No, but after me one is coming, the sandals of whose feet I
am not worthy to untie.'**

²⁶**"Brethren, sons of the family of Abraham, and those
among you that fear God, to us has been sent the message of
this salvation.**

1:32, 69; Rom. 1:3; 2 Tim. 2:8; Rev. 5:5; 22:16 and notes on
Acts 2:29-36). Because the Lord **found in David a man after**
his own **heart** (cf. 1 Sam. 13:14; Ps. 89:20), he elected to
take from **this man's posterity** (cf. 2 Sam. 7:12-16) a **Savior**
for Israel. When the apostle proclaimed that this heir of
David was Jesus, he was appropriating the full weight and
significance of the Old Testament Davidic covenant and
applying it to Jesus.

[**24, 25**] Witness to Jesus' role as Savior is found not
only in God's relationship to David, but also in a more
recent witness, **John** the Baptist. John was a great and
powerful religious figure in first-century Judaism, a man of
conviction, a martyr, a founder of a Jewish sect which lived
past his death. Consequently, John's testimony to Jesus,
even though his disciples were distinct from Jesus' (Luke
5:33; Matt. 9:14; 11:11; Acts 19:1-4; John 3:25), was of value
in preaching to Jewish audiences (cf. Matt. 3:14; John 1:15,
25, 26; 3:30).

Jesus the Fulfillment, 13:26-41. [**26, 27**] This section of
the sermon begins with a restatement of 13:16b, which
identified the audience as sons of **Abraham** and Godfearers.
The first portion of the sermon was connected in the chain
of God's salvation history with Israel. Whereas this salvation history was the focus of the first section (13:17-25), the
second section (13:26-41) is structured around the theme of
prophecy-fulfillment. Accordingly, the apostle's first point is
that Jesus' death, as well as the actions of the inhabitants
and **rulers** of Jerusalem, must be understood in the light of

15

²⁷**For those who live in Jerusalem and their rulers, because they did not recognize him nor understand the utterances of the prophets which are read every sabbath, fulfilled these by condemning him.** ²⁸**Though they could charge him with nothing deserving death, yet they asked Pilate to have him killed.** ²⁹**And when they had fulfilled all that was written of him, they took him down from the tree, and laid him in a tomb.** ³⁰**But God raised him from the dead;** ³¹**and for many days he appeared to those who came up with him from Galilee to Jerusalem, who are now his witnesses to the people.** ³²**And we bring you the good news that what God promised to the fathers,** ³³**this he has fulfilled to us their children by raising Jesus; as also it is written in the second psalm,**

'Thou art my Son,
today I have begotten thee.'

Old Testament prophecies. This emphasis on the rulers' part in Jesus' death immediately brings to mind two earlier passages (3:13; 4:25-27; cf. 2:23 and 1 Cor. 2:8). This text does not explicitly name which **utterances of the prophets** the speaker had in mind, but it may well have been Psalm 2:1, 2 (cf. 4:25, 26; David was considered a prophet, Acts 2:30).

[28, 29] Surely the ideas, if not the words, of Isaiah 53 lie behind the thoughts and events described in 13:28, 29. Jesus' innocent death and the unjust condemnation by Pilate were all foretold. But the prophecies of God did not cease with Jesus slain, interred, and venerated as a martyr.

[30, 31] God **raised** Jesus from a state of death and **corruption,** and Jesus **appeared** (*ōphthē*; cf. Luke 24:34; 1 Cor. 15:5-8; 1 Tim. 3:16) on several occasions **for many days** to his followers who were **with him from Galilee** (cf. Luke 23:49, 55; 24:6). These postresurrection appearances formed the basis of the earliest witnesses (1 Cor. 15:3-8; cf. 1 Cor. 9:1), both men and women.

[32, 33] It is universally recognized that the Old

³⁴And as for the fact that he raised him from the dead, no
more to return to corruption, he spoke in this way,
      'I will give you the holy and sure blessings of David.'
      ³⁵Therefore he says also in another psalm,
      'Thou wilt not let thy Holy One see corruption.'
³⁶For David, after he had served the counsel of God in his own
generation, fell asleep, and was laid with his fathers, and saw
corruption; ³⁷but he whom God raised up saw no corruption.

Testament references to resurrection are not numerous, and
to the resurrection of the Christ himself meager in number.
Jewish sects differed in their views of the resurrection
(Matt. 22:23; Mark 12:18; Luke 20:27; Acts 23:8; 24:21).
How to demonstrate scripturally and authoritatively to a
Jewish audience the prophetic nature of Jesus' resurrection
could have been a formidable obstacle in Paul's message. To
cogently argue his point Paul went not to the Abrahamic or
Mosaic covenants, but to the Old Testament Davidic covenant (13:22, 23). Another glance at Psalm 2 shows how Paul
continued to use it. He may have referred to it earlier in
13:27 (see comments there) and now he explicitly employs
Psalm 2:7 as a proof of Jesus' sonship and ipso facto his
resurrection. Thus these two saving events, namely, Jesus'
unjust execution by the rulers and his receiving of sonship,
are tied by Paul to a prophetic interpretation of the second
psalm. The close connection between Jesus' resurrection
and messianic status is reflected at other places in the New
Testament (e.g., 2:29-36). This doctrinal relationship is
probably best presented in Romans 1:4 when Paul writes
that Jesus Christ "was designated Son of God in power
according to the Spirit of holiness by his resurrection from
the dead." Thus the concept of **today** in 13:33 refers to
resurrection Sunday.

   [34-37] Now a second group of Old Testament verses are
employed by Paul to prove further that Jesus was raised
from the dead, freed forever from mortal **corruption**
(*diaphthora*; cf. 2:27, 31; Ps. 30:9, Greek; cognate *phthar-*

³⁸Let it be known to you therefore, brethren, that through this man forgiveness of sins is proclaimed to you, ³⁹and by him every one that believes is freed from everything from which you could not be freed by the law of Moses.

---

tos, 1 Cor. 15:53f.). Scholars have questioned Paul's joining these two Old Testament verses, Isaiah 55:3 and Psalm 16:10. In what way, it has been asked, does the first verse of Isaiah 55:3 (Greek) correlate with Psalm 16:10? One explanation is that Paul was employing here a well-known Rabbinic method of interpretation called *gezera shewa*, whereby one verse was linked to another solely on the basis of a common term occurring in both. According to this theory the common denominator would be the word **holy** (*hosion*). Another possibility, however, is that Paul believes that the quintessence of the Davidic covenant is its futurity, its looking to a final descendant upon the throne of David (Acts 2:30; cf. 2 Sam. 7:16). The emphasis already given by Paul to promise (13:23), posterity (13:23), and prophecy-fulfillment (13:32, 33) would buttress this interpretation. This futuristic aspect would explain the emphasis upon David as a prophet (Acts 1:16; 2:30, 31; 4:25). Accordingly it would be natural to see the **holy and sure blessings** of David as reaching a culmination in the Lord's resurrection (see notes on Acts 2:27).

[38] For the first time the apostle mentions **forgiveness of sins**. Though he has not yet broached this concept to his audience, it is his way to lead to the ensuing topic of the inadequacy of the Mosaic law. To this juncture the speaker has stressed the continuity between the Old and New Covenants, but now it is time to reveal the superiority of the New over the Old.

[39] Since the Levitical sacrificial system was a part of the Mosaic covenant, it was appropriate for Paul to couch this point in terms of the innate drawbacks to the **law of Moses**. The meaning of this verse has engendered debate.

⁴⁰**Beware, therefore, lest there come upon you what is said in the prophets:**
⁴¹**'Behold, you scoffers, and wonder, and perish;**
  for I do a deed in your days,
  a deed you will never believe, if one declares it to you.' "
⁴²**As they went out, the people begged that these things might be told them the next sabbath.** ⁴³**And when the meeting of the synagogue broke up, many Jews and devout converts to Judaism followed Paul and Barnabas, who spoke to them and urged them to continue in the grace of God.**

Grammatically it could be saying either (1) In Jesus God supplements the partial freedom or acquittal (*dikaiōthēnai*; cf. Rom. 2:13) the law afforded Jews or (2) The Mosaic law is impotent to procure freedom or acquittal (*dikaiōthēnai*; cf. Rom. 3:20; 4:2; 5:1; Gal. 2:16; 3:8, 11, 24) for individuals, and therefore this must be secured exclusively in Jesus. The latter interpretation harmonizes more easily with Paul's doctrine expressed elsewhere and is therefore preferable.

[**40, 41**] Paul knew from his earliest days as a preacher, as well as from his past life (9:23-25; 8:3; 22:4; 26:9-11; 1 Cor. 15:9; Gal. 1:13, 23; Phil. 3:6), the intensity of Jewish opposition to the gospel (1 Thess. 2:14-16). Paul concludes his sermon with a warning against **scoffers** and those who will never believe. The text which he cites from Habakkuk (1:5, Greek) attacks the recalcitrant nature of Jewish disbelief—disbelief in the face of cogent evidence.

The Jewish Response, 13:42-52

[**42**] Since the sabbath was the designated time for synagogal instruction, the crowds urged Paul and Barnabas to return on the **next sabbath**.

[**43**] Paul was apparently satisfied to wait until the next sabbath to instruct them, urging them now only **to continue in the grace** (*charis*) **of God.** Since none of the **Jews** or **devout converts** to Judaism had at this point confessed Jesus as the

⁴⁴The next sabbath almost the whole city gathered together to hear the word of God. ⁴⁵But when the Jews saw the multitudes, they were filled with jealousy, and contradicted what was spoken by Paul, and reviled him. ⁴⁶And Paul and Barnabas spoke out boldly, saying, "It was necessary that the word of God should be spoken first to you. Since you thrust it from you, and judge yourselves unworthy of eternal life, behold, we turn to the Gentiles. ⁴⁷For so the Lord has commanded us, saying,

'I have set you to be a light for the Gentiles,
    that you may bring salvation to the uttermost parts of the earth.' "

Christ, the word **grace** in 13:43 must carry the idea of favor (cf. Luke 2:40; Acts 14:26; 15:40) rather than saving grace. This grace of God was their eagerness to hear again from these apostles of God.

[44, 45] When the Jews who opposed the Christian message saw the multitudes turning to hear Paul's preaching, they were filled with **jealousy** (*zēlos*; cf. 5:17), an attitude which kept the Jews from seeing God's redemptive plan. The intensity of the Jewish attacks is reflected in Luke's use of the terms **contradicted** (*antelegon*; cf. Luke 20:27; Acts 28:19; Titus 2:9 and esp. Luke 2:34; Acts 28:22; Rom. 10:21; Titus 1:9) and **reviled** (*blasphēmeō*; cf. 18:6).

[46, 47] Interpreters have long recognized the importance of 13:46, 47 in attempting to understand Paul's missionary practice and theology. Stated briefly the problem is this: The apostle Paul is designated both in Acts and in his letters as a special apostle, called to preach principally to the Gentiles (Gal. 1:15, 16; 2:7; Rom. 1:5, 13; 1 Tim. 2:7; Acts 9:15; 22:21; 26:16-18). Yet (and this is the apparent enigma) Paul consistently, both in doctrine (Jew first, Rom. 1:16b; 3:1, 2; 9:4, 5) and in practice (9:20; 13:14; 14:1; 17:1; 18:4, 19; 24:12), asserted the priority of the Jews to hear of God's salvation in Christ. Some have sought to explain this problem by suggesting that Luke misconstrued or misunderstood the actions of Paul, thereby leaving a rather blemished picture of the apostle's deeds. This facile explanation will not meet the problem, though, since this tension is present in both Luke's and Paul's writings.

Others have sought to explain Paul's actions on the basis of missionary pragmatism. By this is meant that Paul went to the synagogue in the diaspora because this, pragmatically speaking, was the best way to reach receptive Gentiles. While it is true that the synagogue with its Godfearers and proselytes provided a fertile soil for the word, this approach hardly considers the doctrinal emphasis patent in Paul's statement **It was necessary** (*anankaion*) **that the word of God should be spoken first** (*prōton*; cf. Rom. 1:16; 2:9, 10) **to you.**

The solution to this difficult passage emerges as one follows Paul's reasoning when he cites Isaiah 49:6, as there he boldly unfolds his doctrine about God's plan for the Jewish people in the scheme of redemption and evangelism. God's plan is for the Jews to inherit **eternal life** (*aiōnion zoē*; used only at 13:46, 48 in Acts), but as scoffers they have rejected this when they failed to receive God's actions performed in their midst (13:41). The Jews' mandate from God to witness to the **Gentiles** was abdicated en masse, and only the faithful heirs of Judaism, Jesus (Luke 2:32), and his apostles (13:47) performed this divine task. By abdicating their special role in God's economy the disbelieving Jews **thrust** aside **the word of God** (13:46). The two Jewish missionaries Paul and Barnabas turned to immediate contact with Gentiles since the Jews there could no longer serve as the channel for reaching Gentiles. It is imperative to understand, though, that this action by the apostles did not constitute a wholesale rejection of their Jewish brethren according to the flesh. For throughout the remainder of the Acts it is evident that they habitually went first to the Jewish synagogue in each city (cf. 17:1). On another occasion in Acts Paul denounced Jewish disbelief in a truculent fashion,

⁴⁸**And when the Gentiles heard this, they were glad and glorified the word of God; and as many as were ordained to eternal life believed.** ⁴⁹**And the word of the Lord spread throughout all the region.** ⁵⁰**But the Jews incited the devout women of high standing and the leading men of the city, and stirred up persecution against Paul and Barnabas, and drove them out of their district.** ⁵¹**But they shook off the dust from their feet against them, and went to Iconium.**

---

stating his plan to turn to Gentiles, only to go first to the synagogue in the next locality (cf. 18:6; 28:28). One must conclude then that Paul's modus operandi of "Jew first and then Greek" is a paradigm which applied to each place he preached the word and in no way reflected a midstream shift in practice or thought.

[48] The **Gentiles** rejoiced and **glorified the word of God** (a phrase occurring only here in Acts) when they heard that God's salvation was also available to them. The concepts of **ordained** (*tassō*), appointed, and predestined are rich scriptural ideas (cf. Rom. 8:28, 29; Eph. 1:5, 11; 2 Thess. 2:13; 1 Peter 1:20; Jude 4) when kept free from philosophical or dogmatic interpretations. This verse can as well be translated "As many as believed were appointed to eternal life."

[49] The dissemination of the word **throughout the region** stemmed directly from the commitment of the new believers.

[50] Certain pious aristocratic **women** as well as municipal magistrates were convinced by Jews to oppose the apostles. By driving Paul and Barnabas from the district they hoped to minimize the future threat of urban disturbances engendered by Jewish and Christian hostility (cf. 19:40 and Claudius' expulsion of Jews from Rome for this reason).

[51] Shaking **the dust from their feet** was an indication of contempt for the opponents of the gospel in Antioch (cf. 18:6; Matt. 10:14).

⁵²And the disciples were filled with joy and with the Holy
Spirit.

¹Now at Iconium they entered together into the Jewish
synagogue, and so spoke that a great company believed, both
of Jews and of Greeks. ²But the unbelieving Jews stirred up
the Gentiles and poisoned their minds against the brethren.
³So they remained for a long time, speaking boldly for the
Lord, who bore witness to the word of his grace, granting
signs and wonders to be done by their hands.

---

[52] In spite of the hostile attitude from the people of
Antioch, the disciples exhibited **joy** in the **Spirit** (see notes
on 1:5).

Paul and Barnabas at Iconium, 14:1-7

[1] Since Paul's prior sermon at Pisidian Antioch could
serve as a paradigm of many of his lessons to Jewish
audiences, it was not expedient for Luke to repeat the
details each time. Faith consistently resulted from the
speaking of the word.

[2] Response to the preaching at Iconium was similar to
that elsewhere: A mixed group of **Jews** and Greeks believed;
the sympathies of the city were divided; Jewish leaders
engendered urban unrest among the Gentile rulers.

[3] When speaking boldly for the Lord (*parrēsiazomai*),
Paul and Barnabas exemplified a posture held by other
evangelists and apostles (2:29; 4:13, 29, 31; 9:27, 28; 13:46;
18:26; 19:8; 28:31) and demonstrated that boldness was the
appropriate attitude for any who speak for the Lord and the
word of his grace.

Here, as at Cyprus, the apostles were enabled to per-
form **signs** (*sēmeia*) and **wonders** (*terata*) through **their hands**
(*dia tōn cheirōn autōn*; cf. 5:12; 8:18, 19; 13:11; 14:3;
19:6, 11; 28:8). As was always the case, the purpose of
normative Christian miracles was not to exalt the worker of
wonders, to entertain, or to provide excitement for the
crowds. Luke states that these wonders were to bear **witness**

23

⁴**But the people of the city were divided; some sided with the Jews, and some with the apostles.** ⁵**When an attempt was made by both Gentiles and Jews, with their rulers, to molest them and to stone them,** ⁶**they learned of it and fled to Lystra and Derbe, cities of Lycaonia, and to the surrounding country;** ⁷**and there they preached the gospel.**

⁸**Now at Lystra there was a man sitting, who could not use his feet; he was a cripple from birth, who had never walked.**

(*martureō*; see note on 1:8) **to the word of his grace** (*tō logō tēs charitos autou*; cf. 20:32), just as they had attested to the veracity of Jesus of Nazareth (2:22; cf. Heb. 2:4).

[4] The designation of Barnabas and Paul as **apostles** (*apostoloi*) is cogent evidence that the term *apostle* retained a certain fluidity in its meaning, at least at this juncture in history (cf. 14:14). Barnabas was not one of the twelve (1:21-26; 1 Cor. 15:5), and it is considerably speculative to suggest that he was one of the one hundred and twenty mentioned in Acts 1:15. Had Barnabas been from Galilee he could possibly have been an eyewitness of Jesus' ministry (cf. 1:11; 2:7; 13:31; Luke 23:49, 55; 24:6), but he apparently was not (4:36). In any case, this broader use of the term *apostle*, here equivalent to "missionary," (cf. Rom. 16:7) does not conflict with its narrower use in the New Testament for the twelve and Paul (Matt. 10:2; Mark 3:14; Luke 22:14; Acts 1:26; 5:29.

[5-7] When threatened with stoning and physical abuse, the apostles followed the Lord's mandate (Matt. 10:23) and **fled** to the next town. Although Paul's reflections reveal numerous physical punishments (Gal. 6:17; 2 Cor. 4:10; 11:23-27; Phil. 3:10; Col. 1:24), his demeanor never, unlike certain later martyrs (e.g., Ignatius, the Montanists), showed a morbid proclivity for punishment or death.

Paul and Barnabas at Lystra, 14:8-20

[8] The Roman colony of **Lystra**, discovered less than

⁹**He listened to Paul speaking; and Paul, looking intently at him and seeing that he had faith to be made well,** ¹⁰**said in a loud voice, "Stand upright on your feet." And he sprang up and walked.** ¹¹**And when the crowds saw what Paul had done, they lifted up their voices, saying in Lycaonian, "The gods have come down to us in the likeness of men!"**

---

one century ago, provides the setting for a new facet of Paul's work. In the first place, there is no mention of a synagogue or of any Jews. Moreover, the form of pagan religion here was of a provincial nature. It was neither the mythology of an educated and cultured Sergius Paulus nor an urbane and sophisticated Athenian audience. Rather, it was an expression of rustic simplicity and credulity.

[9, 10] This brief account of Paul's healing miracle at Lystra immediately brings to mind one of Peter's miracles (3:2). The motifs of lame **from birth** (3:2; 14:8), **looking intently** (3:4; 14:9), the command to **stand** and walk (3:6; 14:10), and springing up and walking (3:8; 14:10) are common denominators. The threefold reference by Luke (14:8) to the man's inability to walk provides a dramatic effect. This unnamed individual was made **well** (*sōthēnai*), as usual, on the basis of individual **faith** (*echei pistin*; cf. Matt. 8:5-13; 9:18-22, 27-31; 15:21-28; Mark 5:25-34; 10:46-52; Luke 7:2-10; 7:36-50; 8:43-48; 17:11-19; 18:35-43; Acts 3:11-16; Gal. 3:5; for the power of another's faith see Matt. 9:2; Luke 5:17-26; 1 John 5:13-17), which, in turn, arose from listening to Paul preach. This demonstrates again the close tie between signs and preaching (cf. 13:12; 14:3).

[11] Given the human predilection for signs, wonder-working, theophanies, miracles, etc., the Lycaonian response **(The gods have come down to us in the likeness of men!)** is predictable. In ancient Graeco-Roman times the heavens hung low and the earth was populated with visiting demons and gods (cf. Plato, *Sophist* 216a-b). A locus classicus for this ancient viewpoint is found in Petronius' Latin work of the first century in which one of the characters

[12] **Barnabas they called Zeus, and Paul, because he was the chief speaker, they called Hermes.** [13] **And the priest of Zeus, whose temple was in front of the city, brought oxen and garlands to the gates and wanted to offer sacrifice with the people.**

---

confesses that the "land is so infested with divinity that one might meet a god more easily than a man" (*Satyricon* 17; cf. also Acts 28:6 and Heb. 13:2b).

[**12**] Shouting in their regional archaic tongue of Lycaonian, these crowds responded to this miracle of healing by Paul from a perspective of Graeco-Roman mythology. Thus their claim that Barnabas was **Zeus** and Paul was **Hermes** had a certain mythological matrix in that region of the world. **Zeus** was a father god and **Hermes**, among other things, was the messenger of Zeus. As a messenger of the higher gods Hermes became known as chief of speakers and a leader of communications. The specific myth that provided the historical context to this episode in Acts is probably the Phrygian couple Baucis and Philemon (Ovid's *Metamorphosis* 8. 611-735). The legend recounts how Jupiter (Zeus) and Mercury (Hermes) visited a Phrygian village (Lystra was in Phrygia) disguised as mortal men. Seeking hospitality, they were rejected by thousands of people only to be finally befriended by this poor couple, Baucis and Philemon, who were unaware that these were deities disguised in human likeness. Since they served the gods unknowingly, they were rewarded and everyone else was destroyed. This story was surely known by those at Lystra, and its lesson would readily explain their eagerness to make sure that future visitations of the gods, especially Zeus and Hermes, would not go undetected. (Haenchen's attempts to reject this explanation are typically conjectural and censorious, *The Acts of the Apostles*, pp. 426–434.)

[**13**] F. F. Bruce in his commentary notes that certain late imperial inscriptions from the vicinity of Lystra refer to priests of **Zeus** and the joint worship of Zeus and Hermes

[14]But when the apostles Barnabas and Paul heard of it, they tore their garments and rushed out among the multitude, crying, [15]"Men, why are you doing this? We also are men, of like nature with you, and bring you good news, that you should turn from these vain things to a living God who made the heaven and the earth and the sea and all that is in them.

(pp. 281, 282). Luke's reference to the temple of Zeus **in front of the city** reflects the ancient practice of denominating certain deities and their cults as "before the city" (*pro tēs poleōs*). Sacrifice of **oxen** adorned with **garlands** was a natural response by the **priest of Zeus** to, in his judgment, an epiphany of the deity. This spontaneous response to a theophany is manifest in numerous world religions and can even be documented in examples of patriarchal religion in the Old Testament (Gen. 12:7; 26:24, 25; 35:1, 7, 9-15; Ex. 3:2-6).

[14] From the brevity and structure of Luke's report one cannot know how Paul and Barnabas heard of the attempt to offer sacrifice. Their immediate reaction was to tear their **garments**, thereby showing their protest at this proposed blasphemous act of idolatry (cf. Mark 14:63; Matt. 26:65 for response to blasphemy). The rending of garments was a common sign of protest and sorrow in Judaism (cf. Num. 14:6; 1 Sam. 4:12; 2 Sam. 1:2; 13:31; 15:22; Ezra 9:3-5; Isa. 36:22; Jer. 36:24; 41:5; Joel 2:13).

[15] What follows in verses 15-17 is of singular significance, since it is the first of two sermons in Acts directed solely to a Gentile audience, i.e., to those who had no roots in basic Jewish morality or doctrine. Thus this brief sermon at Lystra, along with the Areopagus message in 17:22-31, preserves a paradigm of how Paul reached out to idolaters. It is also highly informative of how Paul accomplished the task of becoming all things to those "outside the law" (1 Cor. 9:21). Because so many of Paul's converts were previously Gentile idolaters (1 Cor. passim; 1 Thess. 1:9; Gal. 4:8; Eph. 2:11ff.), this example of Paul bringing good

¹⁶ **In past generations he allowed all the nations to walk in their own ways;**

news to Gentile audiences is an essential factor in the grasp of the missionary and evangelistic genius of this great apostle.

By insisting that they were of **like nature** (*homoiopatheis esmen*) with their audience, namely human (*anthrōpoi*) and not gods (*hoi theoi*), the apostles hoped to arrest the Lycaonians' attempt to venerate them. In this address to a Gentile audience Paul yet maintains his roots in Jewish soil, as evident in his dichotomy between the **vain things** (*mataioi*) of heathen idolatry and the **living God** (*theos zōn*) whom he proclaims. This is the first step in bringing the good news to a non-Jewish audience. The Greek word *mataioi* was frequently employed in the Greek Old Testament and early Christian writers (1 Thess. 1:9; Rom. 1:21 for the use of the verb *mataioō*) in their polemics against idolatry. An example of the Jewish argument against idolatry is Isaiah 44:9-20 (cf. Isa. 46:1-7; Wisdom of Solomon 13:1–15:17; Bel and Dragon), where the vanity and absurdity of rejecting a living god for inanimate, reworked, hand-fashioned piece of firewood is graphically stated. The emphasis on the expression **living God** stands out when God is contrasted with the lifeless gods venerated by countless devotees in the Graeco-Roman world. The **living God** whom Paul preached was the Creator (cf. 4:24; 17:24; Gen. 1:1ff.; Ex. 20:11; Neh. 9:6; Ps. 146:6; Isa. 42:5).

[16] God's forbearance in **past generations** is evidenced when he **allowed all nations** to direct their own steps. Unlike the Areopagus sermon (17:30), however, this era of walking **in their own ways** is not explicitly attributed to Gentile ignorance (cf. notes on 3:17). Since the crucial issue of heathen culpability was not raised by Paul at this juncture, the full ramifications of verse 16 are not clear unless verse 16 is to prepare for the contrasting "yet" (*kaitoi*) of verse 17. In this understanding verse 16 would be acknowl-

**yet he did not leave himself without witness, for he did good
and gave you from heaven rains and fruitful seasons, satisfy-
ing your hearts with food and gladness."**

---

edging the Lord's permissiveness (**allowed**, *eiasen*; cf. 16:7;
1 Cor. 10:13) and seeming absence from the sphere of pagan
experience. Verse 17 would then serve to counter the logical
but incorrect conclusion that God was without witness
(*amarturon*, only here in New Testament and never in
Septuagint).

[17] The theme of witnessing permeates the book of
Acts (e.g., 1:8; 2:32; 3:15; 10:39; 10:43; 14:3; 15:8). As the
mandate to witness (1:8) evolves in the Acts of the Apostles,
at each step the witness of God, either through Scripture,
the Spirit, or eyewitnesses to the resurrection, is proclaimed. It is quite consistent with this theme, then, that it
would also play an important role in the proclamation to
Gentile audiences.

Paul's teaching that the realm of nature and the sphere of
natural phenomena are loci of God's revelation is referred to
as natural theology. This concept is also a part of Paul's
Jewish heritage, especially from the Psalter and Old
Testament Wisdom Literature (e.g., Psalms 8; 19; 104; 148).
So here the divine witness available to every human being,
even those not within the tether of God's covenants with
Israel, is proclaimed as manifest in the good benefits God
confers (*agathourgōn*) through rains and fruitful seasons
(cf. Matt. 5:45; Jer. 5:24; Ps. 147:8).

The goal of God's revelation through crops is not solely
to fill the stomach with food, but also the hearts with gladness. A noteworthy parallel to this idea is given in Psalm
145:15, 16, 21:

> The eyes of all look to thee,
> and thou givest them their food in due season.
> Thou openest thy hand,
> thou satisfiest the desire of every living thing.

. . . .

¹⁸ **With these words they scarcely restrained the people from offering sacrifice to them.**

¹⁹ **But Jews came there from Antioch and Iconium; and having persuaded the people, they stoned Paul and dragged him out of the city, supposing that he was dead.** ²⁰ **But when the disciples gathered about him, he rose up and entered the city; and on the next day he went on with Barnabas to Derbe.**

My mouth will speak the praise of the Lord,
   and let all flesh bless his holy name for ever
   and ever.

Though rooted in Jewish thought (the Graeco-Roman philosophical parallels to natural theology will be discussed at Acts 17:22-31), Paul's address to this Gentile audience contained no references, unlike his synagogue sermons, to the Old Testament. Rather, the proof for Paul's sermon here was an affirmation about God's revelation in the experience of the pagan hearers themselves. This modus operandi was assuredly part of Paul's becoming "all things to all men."

[18] Paul's sermon had a counterproductive result. Rather than bringing the hearers to repentance or convicting them to abhor idolatry, it merely reinforced their belief that Paul was, in fact, the god Hermes—a rather paradoxical affirmation to the genius and inspiration of the apostle's preaching.

[19, 20] Luke does not mention a Jewish community at Lystra. Nevertheless **Jews from Antioch and Iconium** tracked Paul and Barnabas there. Paul was pursued by devout Jews who feared, rightly so, the growing influence of Christianity among Jews. So now Paul, previously the hunter (8:3; 9:1, 2, 21; Gal. 1:23), became the hunted. Utilizing a common method of showing anger at someone, stoning, certain people at Lystra attacked the man whom they previously reckoned a god. This particular attempt on Paul's life is prominent in his resume of apostolic credentials—often near death, once stoned, dangers from

²¹**When they had preached the gospel to that city and had made many disciples, they returned to Lystra and to Iconium and to Antioch,** ²²**strengthening the souls of the disciples, exhorting them to continue in the faith, and saying that through many tribulations we must enter the kingdom of God.**

---

my own people (2 Cor. 11:23-26). So vivid was this experience in the life of the apostle that it appeared later in 2 Timothy 3:11, "my persecutions, my sufferings, what befell me at Antioch, at Iconium, and at Lystra, what persecutions I endured." Supposing that Paul was dead, the assailants left his rent body outside the city. Spared once again by the providence of God, the apostle rose up and continued his work (cf. 2 Tim. 3:11c; 4:17c, 18; 2 Cor. 1:8-10; 4:7-12; 7:5, 6; Phil. 2:27).

The Return to Antioch in Syria, 14:21-28

[21] Derbe is scarcely mentioned in Acts and the precise location of the ancient site is still debated. Nevertheless, it was a city where the apostle made many disciples of the gospel. He visited it once again (16:1), and one of his important missionary associates came from there (20:4).

[22] The apostles left Asia Minor by retracing their steps, intentionally passing through Lystra, Iconium, and Antioch. This enabled them to edify and further educate the disciples whom they previously converted. **Strengthening** (*epistērizō*,14:22; 15:32, 41; and *sterizō*, 18:23) and **exhorting** (*parakaleō*, 11:23; 15:32; 16:40; 20:1, 2) were an integral part of Paul's view of his apostolic ministry. He both "planted" and "watered" among numerous congregations in the Roman Empire. And the apostle's own letters provide clear evidence that he never exalted preaching to the detriment of exhortation and strengthening (*sterizō*, Rom. 1:11; 16:25; 1 Thess. 3:2, 13; 2 Thess. 2:17; 3:3; *parakaleō*, Rom. 12:18; 15:30; 16:17; 1 Cor. 1:10; 4:16; 14:31; 2 Cor. 1:3; 14:3; Phil. 2:1; 2 Thess. 2:16).

31

²³And when they had appointed elders for them in every church, with prayer and fasting, they committed them to the Lord in whom they believed.

²⁴Then they passed through Pisidia, and came to Pamphylia. ²⁵And when they had spoken the word in Perga, they went down to Attalia; ²⁶and from there they sailed to Antioch, where they had been commended to the grace of God for the work which they had fulfilled. ²⁷And when they arrived, they gathered the church together and declared all that God had done with them, and how he had opened a door of faith to the Gentiles. ²⁸And they remained no little time with the disciples.

It is little wonder that Paul addressed these believers concerning their tenacity in the faith (*emmenein tē pistei*; for the use of *pistis* meaning the Christian religion cf. Luke 18:8; Acts 6:7; 13:8; 16:5) and their constant encounter with **many tribulations** (*dia pollōn thlipseōn*), for many of these same believers had seen the apostle chased and driven from their own cities as though he and Barnabas were some pestiferous contagion. That small band of believers at Lystra had recently witnessed the apostle's punishment.

Kingdom of God is an infrequent expression in Paul's letters. It usually has, as here, a futuristic eschatological emphasis when he does employ it (1 Cor. 6:9, 10; 15:50; Gal. 5:21; 2 Thess. 1:4, 5).

[23] Attendant to the growth and strengthening of congregations was the appointment of **elders** (*presbuteroi*; cf. 11:30; 15:2-23; 16:4; 20:17; 21:18?; 1 Tim. 5:1, 2, 17, 19; Titus 1:5; James 5:14; 1 Peter 5:5?; 2 John 1; 3 John 1). They **appointed** (*cheirotonēsantes*) these leaders at **every church**, perhaps based on the model of Jewish institutions (see part 1 on 11:30). For the religious use of the term **committed** (*paratithēmi*) see 20:32; 1 Timothy 1:18; 2 Timothy 2:2; 1 Peter 4:19.

[24-28] They continued to retrace their steps as they journeyed homeward to Antioch. Noteworthy is the sugges-

¹But some men came down from Judea and were teaching the brethren, "Unless you are circumcised according to the custom of Moses, you cannot be saved." ²And when Paul and Barnabas had no small dissension and debate with them, Paul and Barnabas and some of the others were appointed to go up to Jerusalem to the apostles and the elders about this question.

---

tion that the word was not preached in Perga when they first entered Asia Minor (13:13, 14) but only as they left (14:25). Perhaps the dispute concerning John Mark was to blame for this. A missionary report of sorts (cf. 11:18; 15:4) was given by the apostles upon their arrival in Antioch, declaring **all that God had done with them** (*met' autōn*). An awareness of divine help permeates the book of Acts and New Testament (cf. 2 Cor. 4:7ff.; 6:1; 1 Cor. 3:9, *theou sunergoi*; Phil. 2:13, *theos ho energōn en humin*). The church at Antioch knew that the growth of the faith as well as the open door of faith (*thura pisteōs*; cf. 1 Cor. 16:9; 2 Cor. 2:12; Col. 4:3) to the Gentiles was possible through God's direction.

THE CONFERENCE IN JERUSALEM, 15:1-35

[1] The indefinite **some men** refers to Christians who were also members of the party of the Pharisees (Acts 15:5). In other places they are called "believers from among the circumcised" (Acts 10:45) and "the circumcision party" (11:2; Gal. 2:12). These taught that table fellowship with Gentiles was forbidden and circumcision was necessary (Gal. 2:12ff.; 5:1ff.).

[2] **Paul and Barnabas** did not submit to the Judean legalists, but decided to travel **to Jerusalem** to confer with the **apostles and elders** in order to resolve the **question** and its implications. According to the Lukan narrative this was the apostle's third visit **to Jerusalem**. Chronologically, the first visit (Acts 9:26) was also that one described by Paul in Galatians 1:18-24; the second (Acts 11:29; 12:25) was

³So, being sent on their way by the church, they passed through both Phoenicia and Samaria, reporting the conversation of the Gentiles, and they gave great joy to all the brethren. ⁴When they came to Jerusalem, they were welcomed by the church and the apostles and the elders, and they declared all that God had done with them. ⁵But some believers who belonged to the party of the Pharisees rose up, and said, "It is necessary to circumcise them, and to charge them to keep the law of Moses."

⁶The apostles and the elders were gathered together to consider this matter.

---

described in Galatians 2:1-10. Thus this third visit to Jerusalem was after Paul founded the churches of south Galatia (Acts 13–14), though perhaps before he wrote his epistle to them.

[3, 4] Perhaps to strengthen their position with other believers they reported **the conversation of the Gentiles** to the believers in **Phoenicia and Samaria**. They continued even in **Jerusalem** to declare what **God had done** (cf. 11:18 and notes on Acts 14:27). It is notable that the **Jerusalem church** functioned under the rule of **elders** (see note on 20:17ff.). These received the relief fund (11:30) and were always mentioned alongside the **apostles** in **Jerusalem** (Acts 15:2, 4, 6, 22, 23; 16:4) in regard to decision making.

[5] The slogan of the legalistic brethren was repeated by Luke (cf. 15:1). It meant that Gentile believers had to be circumcised and adopt Jewish customs in order to be saved. This same issue may have been a problem of disagreement even among various schools of thought in Judaism itself. As Jews tried to convert Gentiles to Judaism, some thought circumcision was more important than others did (see especially Josephus, *Antiquities* XX.ii.3-5). It seems unlikely that the opponents mentioned in Acts 15:1 were substantially different from those mentioned in Acts 15:5.

[6] Since the trouble stemmed from the Jerusalem church (cf. Gal. 2:12, men from James, for a similar situa-

⁷**And after there had been much debate, Peter rose and said to them, "Brethren, you know that in the early days God made choice among you, that by my mouth the Gentiles should hear the word of the gospel and believe.** ⁸**And God who knows the heart bore witness to them, giving them the Holy Spirit just as he did to us;** ⁹**and he made no distinction between us and them, but cleansed their hearts by faith.**

---

tion), **the elders** there reasoned and legislated with **the apostles** (cf. 16:4).

[7] It was not unusual that **Peter** came forward to defend the Gentile mission. The episode with Cornelius (Acts 10:1–11:18) in addition to Paul's testimony (Gal. 2:14-16) reveals that **Peter** at this point was committed to it. His actions might not always be in harmony with his beliefs (Gal. 2:13), but he surely agreed with Paul's doctrine of the acceptability of **the Gentiles**.

[8] This was the second time Luke used the word *kardiognōstēs* (**knows the heart**; Acts 1:24; cf. Luke 16:15). The **heart** (*kardia*) motif was used also by Paul as a way to combat destructive manifestations of Jewish Christianity. This allowed the Christian to distinguish between external Jewish requirements and what **God** required of Gentiles (see especially Rom. 2:25-29). Equally important was the concept that **God** himself had given testimony to the validity of the Gentile mission. This was manifested in the **giving** of **the Holy Spirit**. The combination of the Holy Spirit and the Gentile mission is a theme of Acts (1:4-8; 2:1-21; 8:39; 10:44-48; 11:15-18; 13:2; 15:28; 28:25-28).

[9] The expression **no distinction** was parallel to the belief that God was no respecter of persons (Acts 10:34; Rom. 2:11; Eph. 6:9; Col. 3:25). The common denominator between Jew and Gentile in terms of salvation was the state of the heart. Both Testaments assert that God acknowledges only religious commitment which is rooted in one's heart. A **cleansed** heart, therefore, was the first requirement for salvation (important passages on this concept include

¹⁰**Now therefore why do you make trial of God by putting a yoke upon the neck of the disciples which neither our fathers nor we have been able to bear? ¹¹But we believe that we shall be saved through the grace of the Lord Jesus, just as they will."**

Deut. 6:4-6; 10:12; 11:18; 26:16; 30:2, 14; 32:46; Matt. 5:8; 15:18, 19; Luke 2:35; 6:45; 12:34; 16:15; Rom. 6:17; 8:27).

[10] The language of tempting **God** (*peirazō ton theon*) derives from the Old Testament wilderness account. There it meant acting from disbelief against the clear will of God to the point of breaking his forbearance (Ex. 17:2, 7; Num. 14:22; Ps. 95:9). The psalmist described it as "they tested God in their heart" (Ps. 78:18). The **trial** was manifest in putting an unbearable **yoke** (*zugon*) on the believers. Of course the Mosaic law was never intended to be unbearable. On the contrary, it was an object of delight (Ps. 19:7-10; Ps. 119:1-176). As Paul wrote, "the law is holy, and the commandment is holy and just and good," and "we know that the law is spiritual" (Rom. 7:12, 14). In fact Moses taught that if the Lord's word was in a person's heart, the commandment was not too hard for him to keep (Deut. 30:11-14). Unfortunately, sin turned God's Torah into man's statutes, thereby making it a **yoke** of slavery (Gal. 5:1). On **yoke** as referring to teaching, compare the words from Matthew "take my yoke upon you. For my yoke is easy" (Matt. 11:29, 30). The united testimony of Jewish history and scripture is that the **fathers** were unable **to bear** this burden.

[11] Two points are brought together here. The first is a central teaching in the New Testament, namely, that salvation is **through the grace of the Lord Jesus** (e.g., Rom. 3:24; 4:16; 5:15, 17, 20; 6:14; Gal. 1:6, 15; Eph. 1:7; 2:5, 8; 3:2; Titus 3:7). Second, **just as** it came to the Jews, so it came also to the Gentiles; there is only one source of salvation. As Paul was to express it in another place, God is the God of the Gentiles also since God is one (Rom. 3:29, 30).

¹² And all the assembly kept silence; and they listened to
Barnabas and Paul as they related what signs and wonders
God had done through them among the Gentiles. ¹³ After they
finished speaking, **James** replied, "Brethren, listen to me.
¹⁴Simeon has related how God first visited the Gentiles, to
take out of them a people for his name.

---

[12] Cephas' forceful argument produced **silence** and
ended the debate (15:7). **Barnabas and Paul** then reported
upon their own proof for the truth of the Gentile mission.
These **signs** (*sēmeia*) and **wonders** (*terata*) were offered as
proof of God's presence among the missionaries themselves. It does not say that the Gentiles worked these
miracles. In the case of Cornelius his ability to speak in
tongues verified God's approval of **Gentiles** (Acts 10:46, 47).
Here, however, the **signs and wonders** may have been to
verify the apostolic Gentile ministry of Paul (1 Cor. 12:12).

[13] This **James** was the brother of the Lord (cf. Acts
12:17; 21:18; 1 Cor. 15:7; Gal. 1:19; 2:9, 12) who was killed
in Jerusalem in A.D. 62 for siding with progressive Jewish
Christianity (Josephus, *Antiquities* XX. ix. 1; cf. Eusebius,
Ecclesiastical History II. 23). Another James, who was one
of the twelve, died under Agrippa I (Acts 12:2).

[14] James appealed to the testimony of **Simeon**
(i.e., Peter) that **God** had **visited the Gentiles**. The Greek
word *episkeptomai*, translated **visited**, was specifically used
at times to relate God's salvific visitation. Its Jewish roots in
the Greek Old Testament are seen in instances such as "The
Lord visited Sarah" (Gen. 21:1, 2); "God will visit you and
bring you up out of this land" (Gen. 50:24); or "The Lord
visited his people and gave them food" (Ruth 1:6;
cf. Ex. 4:31). In the New Testament it was used messiani-
cally in the following examples: Zechariah prophesied "The
Lord God of Israel has visited and redeemed his people"
(Luke 1:67, 68; cf. 1:78); one of Jesus' miracles was followed by the exclamation "God has visited his people"
(Luke 7:16).

[15] And with this the words of the prophets agree, as it is written,

[16] 'After this I will return,
and I will rebuild the dwelling of David, which has fallen;
I will rebuild its ruins, and I will set it up,

[17] that the rest of men may seek the Lord, and all the Gentiles who are called by my name,

[18] says the Lord, who has made these things known from of old.'

[19] Therefore my judgment is that we should not trouble those of the Gentiles who turn to God, [20] but should write to them to abstain from the pollutions of idols and from unchastity and from what is strangled[n] and from blood.

[n] Other early authorities omit *and from what is strangled*

Consequently, the concept of visiting the **Gentiles** meant the universality of salvation (a use of *episkeptomai* found only in Luke in the New Testament). The term **people** (*laos*) was also highly significant. It frequently was used to designate Israel, while *ethnē* was employed to designate **Gentiles** (e.g., Acts 4:24ff.; 12:4; 21:28). We thus see James teaching that the prized term *laos* (**people**) was now to be applied not only to Israel but also to Gentile Christians (cf. Rom. 9:24; Acts 18:10; Titus 2:14; 1 Peter 2:9).

[15-18] In this section James proved that the Old Testament **prophets** (Amos 9:11f. in the Greek Old Testament) substantiated this understanding. The rebuilding of **the dwelling of David** meant the hoped-for restoration of Israel prior to the influx of Gentiles. This concept was clearly a part of Old Testament messianism (especially Isa. 49:6; 2:2-4; 42:6; Zech. 2:11). That God must deal with Israel first and then the **Gentiles** was also proclaimed by Paul in his sermon at Pisidian Antioch (Acts 13:46, 47 and notes there) and in Romans (1:16; 2:10).

[19, 20] It was the **judgment** of James, then, that Israel was the means to an end and not the end itself. That is, it was to point **Gentiles to God** and not to itself. Consequently,

[21] For from early generations Moses has had in every city those who preach him, for he is read every sabbath in the synagogues."

Gentile Christians should not be troubled (same term used in Gal. 1:7; 5:10 for disruptions caused by legalistic Christianity). Rather than their being required to be circumcised and keep the law of Moses (15:1, 5), James resolved that the conflict could be settled by Gentiles abstaining from: (1) **pollutions of idols,** (2) **unchastity** (*porneia*), (3) **what is strangled,** and (4) **blood. Pollutions of idols** referred to food offered to **idols,** as Acts 15:29 and 21:25 make clear. According to many scholars these four stipulations represent the so-called Noachic Code, i.e., laws given to Noah for *all mankind* to observe. Observation of these laws was required of Gentiles who wished to attend the synagogue regularly without becoming proselytes to Judaism. On this reading the decision reached at the Jerusalem conference was in the nature of a compromise. In any case, since this decree was not destined for the western part of the Roman Empire (Acts 15:23; 16:4), the Corinthian Gentile Christians could eat meats presented to idols so long as no situation similar to Acts 15 (i.e., weaker brethren) developed (1 Cor. 8:1ff.). **Unchastity** was also forbidden. This might have been in reference to certain Jewish understandings of marital laws and sexual taboos (e.g., Lev. 18). On the other hand, it might have been part of the list because of the frequent association between sexual immorality and pagan temples. Jewish law plainly forbade eating an animal's **blood,** a condition which happened when an animal was **strangled** (cf. Lev. 17:10ff.).

[21] Summarized speeches always leave room for questions. This is especially true of James' speech. How, for example, did his solution fully respond to the issues raised by the Pharisaic believers (15:1, 5)? Moreover, how does his statement about **Moses** being preached **in synagogues** relate to the rest of his talk?

²²Then it seemed good to the apostles and the elders, with the whole church, to choose men from among them and send them to Antioch with Paul and Barnabas. They sent Judas called Barsabbas, and Silas, leading men among the brethren, ²³with the following letter: "The brethren, both the apostles and the elders, to the brethren who are of the Gentiles in Antioch and Syria and Cilicia, greeting. ²⁴Since we have heard that some persons from us have troubled you with words, unsettling your minds, although we gave them no instructions, ²⁵it has seemed good to us, having come to one accord, to choose men and send them to you with our beloved Barnabas and Paul, ²⁶men who have risked their lives for the sake of our Lord Jesus Christ. ²⁷We have therefore sent Judas and Silas, who themselves will tell you the same things by word of mouth. ²⁸For it has seemed good to the Holy Spirit and to us to lay upon you no greater burden than these necessary things: ²⁹that you abstain from what has been sacrificed to idols and from blood and from what is strangled ⁿ and from unchastity. If you keep yourselves from these, you will do well. Farewell."

ⁿ Other early authorities omit *and from what is strangled*

Moses was preached in the form of expositions based upon the Pentateuch. The regularity of **sabbath** instruction was well known throughout the Roman Empire. Philo called this instruction a school of practical wisdom which assembled every seventh day (*Special Laws* II.15; see also notes on Acts 13:14ff.).

[22] The decision was made to circulate this official decree. The nature of the regulations was decided by the **apostles**. The resolution concerning how to send the letter was reached by the **apostles** and **elders with** their **church**. Returning to **Antioch** with **Paul** and **Barnabas** were **Judas and Silas**.

[23-29] A **letter** was **sent** out to inform certain churches about this decision. Ostensibly the regulations would be

³⁰**So when they were sent off, they went down to Antioch;
and having gathered the congregation together, they delivered
the letter.** ³¹**And when they read it, they rejoiced at the
exhortation.** ³²**And Judas and Silas, who were themselves
prophets, exhorted the brethren with many words and
strengthened them.**

---

binding upon **Gentiles in Antioch, Syria**, and **Cilicia**. The
letter patently disavowed any sympathy for those legalistic
brethren who **troubled** and unsettled Gentile converts
(cf. Gal. 1:7; 5:10). In addition, the letter depicted a final
harmony, **one accord**, among the apostles and Paul.

The reference to the **Holy Spirit** showed the divine
wisdom reflected in the decision (cf. Acts 13:2; 16:6 for the
Spirit's operation in missionary matters). The four above-
mentioned regulations were considered as **things necessary**.
The immediate question is **necessary** for what. Were they
necessary for unity, for love, or for salvation? That is, does
James believe that the "grace of the Lord Jesus" (15:11) was
not enough? Does he, after all, agree with the circumcision
party in principle having only a different list of requirements? Apparently not, since this would hardly be in **one
accord** with the earlier message of Peter (15:7-11). If it had
been **necessary** for salvation, its relevance would have been
greater than for only three provinces. Verse 29 repeats in a
different order the items in verse 20.

[**30**] Paul, Barnabas, Judas, and Silas returned **to
Antioch** to deliver **the letter**. Similar to the practice in
Pauline churches the whole **congregation**, not just the
bishops, was present when the **letter** was read (see especially 1 Thess. 5:27; Col. 4:16).

[**31, 32**] The Antioch Gentiles **rejoiced** at this victory
over those who came preaching justification by works of
law, i.e., circumcision (Acts 15:1). **Exhortation** and
strengthening may have been part of **Judas and Silas'**
prophetic task (see notes on 14:22). This agrees with the
work of prophets described in 1 Corinthians 14:3.

³³And after they had spent some time, they were sent off in peace by the brethren to those who had sent them.* ³⁵But Paul and Barnabas remained in Antioch, teaching and preaching the word of the Lord, with many others also.

³⁶And after some days Paul said to Barnabas, "Come, let us return and visit the brethren in every city where we proclaimed the word of the Lord, and see how they are." ³⁷And Barnabas wanted to take with them John called Mark. ³⁸But Paul thought best not to take with them one who had withdrawn from them in Pamphylia, and had not gone with them to the work. ³⁹And there arose a sharp contention, so that they separated from each other; Barnabas took Mark with him and sailed away to Cyprus, ⁴⁰but Paul chose Silas and departed, being commended by the brethren to the grace of the Lord. ⁴¹And he went through Syria and Cilicia, strengthening the churches.

*Other ancient authorities insert verse 34, *But it seemed good to Silas to remain there*

[33-35] After a ministry in Antioch these prophets returned **in peace** to Jerusalem. **Paul and Barnabas remained** there **teaching and preaching the word**. This scene ends with a peaceful relationship among the three figures of **Paul**, James, and Peter (cf. 21:17, 18; Gal. 2:9).

PAUL'S SECOND JOURNEY, 15:36–18:21

Preparations, 15:36-41

[36] Plans were made by the apostle **Paul** to begin his so-called second missionary journey. It was ostensibly a journey for edifying previous converts. By the Lord's direction it was to develop into something much larger.

[37, 38] **Barnabas** wanted **Mark** to accompany them. Paul, reflecting upon **John Mark**'s earlier desertion **in Pamphylia** (Acts 13:13), rejected the idea.

[39-41] The disagreement between **Barnabas** and **Paul** could not be satisfactorily resolved. Consequently they

¹And he came also to Derbe and to Lystra. A disciple was there, named Timothy, the son of a Jewish woman who was a believer; but his father was a Greek. ²He was well spoken of by the brethren at Lystra and Iconium. ³Paul wanted Timothy to accompany him; and he took him and circumcised him because of the Jews that were in those places, for they all knew that his father was a Greek.

---

went their separate ways. **Paul and Silas** (who had returned from Jerusalem) went through **Syria** and Turkey while **Barnabas** and **Mark** sailed **to Cyprus**. This is the last reference to **Barnabas** in Acts. However, since he was well known by the Christians in Corinth (1 Cor. 9:6), he may have joined Paul later on the second journey when the Corinthian church was established (Acts 18:5ff.).

Return to Asia Minor, 16:1-10

[1, 2] Paul once again was among the Galatian churches, accompanied this time by Silas rather than Barnabas (15:39, 40). At **Lystra** he met **Timothy**, soon to become a distinguished protege, emissary, and coauthor with Paul (Rom. 16:21; 1 Cor. 4:17; 16:10; 2 Cor. 1:1, 19; Phil. 1:1; Col. 1:1; 1 Thess. 1:1; 3:2; 2 Thess. 1:1; 1 Tim. 1:2, 18; 2 Tim. 1:2; Phile. 1). Timothy's mother was also a Christian (cf. 2 Tim. 1:5), though we cannot be certain of the exact circumstances of his conversion (cf. 2 Tim. 3:15). Although Timothy's mother was **Jewish**, she apparently quite assimilated her Hellenistic environs since the text of Acts reports that her husband was a **Greek**, and Timothy remained uncircumcised in his infancy. This type of casual attitude toward circumcision among mixed marriages is attested in Hellenistic Jewish writings of that era. That Timothy was **well spoken of** (for this use of *martureō* cf. 6:3; 10:22; 22:12; 1 Tim. 5:10; Heb. 11:2) by the brothers made him an asset in Paul's work.

[3] Paul's sensitivity to the Jewish acceptability of Timothy was embodied in his decision to have him **circum-**

43

⁴As they went on their way through the cities, they delivered to them for observance the decisions which had been reached by the apostles and elders who were at Jerusalem. ⁵So the churches were strengthened in the faith, and they increased in numbers daily.

⁶And they went through the region of Phrygia and Galatia, having been forbidden by the Holy Spirit to speak the word in Asia. ⁷And when they had come opposite Mysia, they attempted to go into Bithynia, but the Spirit of Jesus did not allow them; ⁸so, passing by Mysia, they went down to Troas.

---

cised. There is no valid reason to impugn the accuracy of this description of Paul's actions. In the first place, Paul himself confesses that to reach those "under the law" he became "as one under the law" (1 Cor. 9:20). Moreover, even in his fiercest denunciation of circumcision being required of Christians (Gal. 2:3; 5:2-6) Paul admitted (with Timothy in mind?) that on occasion he "preached circumcision" (Gal. 5:11). Paul, however, unlike his Galatian opponents, was seeking to expedite missionary work by making Timothy (a half-Jew) more acceptable to Jewish audiences. The text of Acts explicitly states that it was **because of the Jews** that Paul circumcised Timothy. It was clearly not because Paul believed, "unless you are circumcised according to the custom of Moses, you cannot be saved" (15:1).

[4, 5] Paul and Silas distributed the Jerusalem decisions (*dogmata*) reached at the prior conference (ch. 15) to the cities in Galatia. Although the original decrees were for the churches in Antioch, Syria, and Cilicia only, they went also to Galatia because these churches were, in effect, missionary extensions of the Antioch church. A summary concluding this section notes the spiritual growth as well as numerical growth of the faith. This type of summary statement is used elsewhere by Luke to end one section and move into another (cf. 6:7; 9:31).

[6-8] This brief section serves as a transition from the end of Paul's trip across Asia Minor to the beginning of his

⁹And a vision appeared to Paul in the night: a man of
Macedonia was standing beseeching him and saying, "Come
over to Macedonia and help us." ¹⁰And when he had seen the
vision, immediately we sought to go on into Macedonia,
concluding that God had called us to preach the gospel to
them.
    ¹¹Setting sail therefore from Troas, we made a direct
voyage to Samothrace, and the following day to Neapolis,

---

work in Greece. He and Silas were **forbidden by the
Holy Spirit** to evangelize **Asia**, the leading and most prosper-
ous province in the eastern Roman Empire. The concrete
way in which this prohibition of the Spirit was shown is not
revealed in Scripture. Only later was the door to Asia
opened for the apostle (ch. 19), and then it became the site
of his longest and most successful missionary work (19:10;
20:31). The **Spirit of Jesus** also kept them out of **Bithynia**, the
later site of numerous churches probably established by
Peter (1 Peter 1:1).

    [9, 10] While at the city of Troas, a Roman colony in the
northwest section of Asia Minor, Paul received a nighttime
vision. The city of Troas is mentioned both in Acts (20:5, 6)
and Paul's letters (2 Cor. 2:12; 2 Tim. 4:13). Christian vi-
sions (*horama*, Acts 9:10-12; 10:3, 17, 19; 11:5; 12:9; 18:9;
cf. *horasis*, Acts 2:17; 22:17; Col. 2:18; Rev. passim) were
often media for the revelation of God's will. A Macedonian
besought Paul in this vision to come to **Macedonia**, the
northern section of Greece, to assist them by the preaching
of the gospel. Paul recognized this as a directive from God.
It is unlikely that the man in the vision was Luke, as
Ramsay suggests, since Luke was with Paul in Troas. This is
known because the "we" passages begin while Paul was in
Troas.

Paul and Silas at Philippi, 16:11-40

    Lydia, the First Convert in Europe, 16:11-15. [11, 12] In
the transit from Asia Minor to Europe, Paul and his com-

45

¹²and from there to Philippi, which is the leading city of the district* of Macedonia, and a Roman colony. We remained in this city some days; ¹³and on the sabbath day we went outside the gate to the riverside, where we supposed there was a place of prayer; and we sat down and spoke to the women who had come together.

* The Greek text is uncertain

---

panions stayed one night in **Samothrace**. The student interested in Graeco-Roman religious backgrounds of the New Testament could only wish that Luke had preserved some episode or facts about this small but important island home of the Samothracian gods and mysteries. **Neapolis**, port city of Philippi, was situated on the famous Via Egnatia, an important Roman interprovincial highway to the east.

[12] **Philippi** is correctly designated by Luke as both a **leading city** (though not the capital) in Macedonia as well as a **Roman colony**. In regard to the latter, F. F. Bruce observed (*Acts of the Apostles*, p. 313): "A Roman colony was like a piece of Rome or Italy transplanted abroad; its citizens enjoyed the same rights as they have had in Italy." Like other Roman colonies mentioned by Luke (e.g., Pisidian Antioch, Lystra, Troas, Corinth) Philippi enjoyed the liberty of autonomous rule, immunity from taxes and tribute, and the laws of Italian Romans. Such strong colony sentiment helps explain an episode at Philippi later mentioned by Luke (see notes on 16:21).

[13] Reference to the **sabbath day** demonstrates that the missionaries were searching out a Jewish group. But rather than the practice of attending a synagogue, the search was for a **place of prayer**. The Greek word here (*proseuchē*) could refer to a Jewish synagogue, but it is unlikely since only women are mentioned, and men—in fact ten—were required for a synagogue. The missionaries supposed there would be a worship site by the riverside, because often Jews and Godfearers would pray by seashore and riverside when

¹⁴**One who heard us was a woman named Lydia, from the city of Thyatira, a seller of purple goods, who was a worshiper of God. The Lord opened her heart to give heed to what was said by Paul. ¹⁵ And when she was baptized, with her household, she besought us, saying, "If you have judged me to be faithful to the Lord, come to my house and stay." And she prevailed upon us.**

---

having no access to a synagogue (cf. Ps. 137:1; Ezra 8:15, 21). Women were on equal standing with men in the early church in regard to the availability of salvation (2:17, 18; Gal. 3:28).

[14] Lydia's interest in the gospel is another example of Luke's desire to show that the word of God was received by wealthy and aristocratic individuals of the Roman world. **Thyatira** (cf. Rev. 2:19-29) was a city in the Anatolian region of Lydia, ironically not far from where Paul received the call to come to Macedonia (16:8-10). The city was famous since early times for its trade in purple dyes and goods (Homer, *Iliad* 4.141f.; Strabo *Geography* 13.4-14), and epigraphical remains attest the existence of dye-guilds in ancient Thyatira. Since a heart must be opened to receive the Christian message (cf. Luke 8:12; Acts 2:37; 8:21, 22; 13:22; 15:9; 28:27), God **opened** the **heart** of this truth seeker. The expression "God opened the heart" is found in Luke 24:45 but nowhere else in regard to conversions. It is significant that this opening of the heart came only after she heard what was said by Paul. Perhaps the method of opening her heart was the preached word (cf. Luke 24:45).

While a Macedonian man may have motivated Paul to travel to Macedonia, the Lord's first converts there (see note on 16:40) were Asian women. Highly noteworthy is Paul's statement in Philippians that certain women "labored side by side with me in the gospel" (Phil. 4:2).

[15] The unusual thing in regard to Lydia's baptism is that **her household** was baptized with her. Apparently she

¹⁶ **As we were going to the place of prayer, we were met by a slave girl who had a spirit of divination and brought her owners much gain by soothsaying.**

---

was unmarried, widowed, or divorced. That the Greek term *oikos* (**household**; cf. 11:14; 16:15, 33; 18:8; 1 Cor. 1:16; 16:15, 16) cannot cogently support the theories of Paedobaptists has been forcefully and succinctly demonstrated by G. R. Beasley-Murray, *Baptism in the New Testament* (pp. 312–320). Immediately following her conversion Lydia prevailed upon Paul and the others to accept her hospitality as proof of their acceptance of her. A practice in the early church was for Christians to keep other Christians in their homes (cf. 9:43; 10:6; 16:34; 17:5; 18:7; 21:16; Heb. 13:1, 2; 3 John 5-8; *Didache* 11-12), and hospitality (*philoxenia*, Rom. 12:13; 1 Tim. 3:2; Titus 1:8; 1 Peter 4:9) was considered more than an optional social grace.

Divination at Philippi, 16:16-18. [16] This curious vignette sounds strange in the modern reader's hearing since it is rooted so thoroughly in the oft forgotten soil of ancient divination and the world of the occult. As Paul and Luke were making their way to the usual place of prayer, they encountered a **slave girl** who served as a medium or ventriloquist for a spirit of sorcery. Luke writes that she had a **spirit of divination** (*pneuma pythona*). The Greek term *pythona* is the source of our English word *python* (and in Greek mythology Python was the particular snake slain at Delphi by Apollo). To recapitulate the mythic background of this pagan belief, it was held that the female oracle, prophetess, or medium at the famous site of Delphi in Greece had a spirit living in her body which could foretell the future, and this it would do by seizing control, often violently, of the female oracle's voice. Thus the prophetess would lose control of herself and become for the duration of the prophecy a mere medium or dummy in the hands of the spirit of divination (contrast the Christian understanding of prophecy in 1 Cor. 14:32). Pagan oracles existed every-

[17] She followed Paul and us, crying, "These men are servants of the Most High God, who proclaim to you the way of salvation." [18] And this she did for many days. But Paul was annoyed, and turned and said to the spirit, "I charge you in the name of Jesus Christ to come out of her." And it came out that very hour.

---

where in the Graeco-Roman world and this spirit of possession, wherever it might appear, was frequently called in a generic fashion the "pythian spirit" or, as the RSV states, the **spirit of divination**. Since customarily pagan oracles, soothsaying, and prophecies were given for remuneration (cf. 8:18-22), the owners of this slave girl could easily receive **much gain** from such huckstering.

[17] During certain periods of her seizures she would exclaim, **These men are servants of the Most High God, who proclaim to you the way of salvation**. The most obvious question that comes to the mind of the reader is why the possessed girl endorsed the God and message of the Christian missionaries. In an attempt to answer this rather enigmatic problem it must first be pointed out that the term **Most High God** "was a divine title current among both Jews and Greeks, and thus provided them with a common denominator in referring to the Deity" (Bruce, p. 315). Second, both the Old and New Testaments put forth the concept that in the spirit world of darkness and the occult these spirits knew the reality of God's power and at times confessed it. One only need read the Balaam oracles in Numbers (23–24) or the demonic confessions in the Synoptic Gospels (Mark 5:7; Luke 4:34, 41; 8:28) to perceive this pattern (cf. Acts 19:15; Phil. 2:10; James 2:19).

The term **way** in Acts is sometimes a synonym for Christianity (9:2; 19:9, 23; 24:22). The expression **way of salvation,** however, is found only here in the New Testament.

[18] Paul became **annoyed** at this repetitive incident, perhaps because of the duplicity and hypocrisy it evi-

[19] But when her owners saw that their hope of gain was gone, they seized Paul and Silas and dragged them into the market place before the rulers; [20] and when they had brought them to the magistrates they said, "These men are Jews and they are disturbing our city. [21] They advocate customs which it is not lawful for us Romans to accept or practice."

---

denced. Or perhaps he was outraged by the possible link in some people's minds between his message and pagan oracular possession. In any case, after **many days** he exorcised the spirit **in the name of Jesus Christ** (for the significance of the name of Jesus in miracles and exorcisms, cf. Matt. 7:22; Mark 9:38, 39; Luke 10:17; Acts 3:6, 16; Phil. 2:10). Luke omitted further information about this nameless slave girl and whether, when freed, she accepted the way of salvation which the evil spirit spoke through her.

Litigation and Imprisonment at Philippi, 16:19-24. [19] This is the first urban disruption by Gentile fomenters in Acts. Up to this point Jewish hostility was usually the catalyst for frequent riots and civil disturbances in the wake of Paul. Here the owners decided to attack Paul. And the reason for this attack was that their source of income had dried up and their **hope of gain** (cf. 16:16) was gone. Paul and Silas were **dragged into the market place** (*agora*) for the formal charge **before the rulers** (*archontes*), who had the power to administer limited personal punishments. These rulers are identical with the magistrates (*stratēgoi*) in verse 20.

[20, 21] The anti-Semitism implicit in the statement **These men are Jews** is incontestable. Notwithstanding the fact that Judaism was a legal religion in the Empire, there were intense ethnic and cultural prejudices which sporadically erupted between Jew and Gentile. The charge that Christians were guilty of fomenting urban unrest and disturbing the city was made more than once against early Christians. And there was truth to the charge insofar as the gospel's message frequently flew in the face of many urban

²²The crowd joined in attacking them; and the magistrates tore the garments off them and gave orders to beat them with rods. ²³And when they had inflicted many blows upon them, they threw them into prison, charging the jailer to keep them safely. ²⁴Having received this charge, he put them into the inner prison and fastened their feet in the stocks.

²⁵But about midnight Paul and Silas were praying and singing hymns to God, and the prisoners were listening to them,

---

practices, mores, and attitudes. The closest thing to the charge of advocating unlawful customs would have been the conversion of a Roman citizen to specious Eastern cults or Judaism, and this is exactly how many viewed early Christianity. In this particular instance the idea was that Paul and others were attempting to gain converts to Judaism. Imperial writers such as Horace and Juvenal depict a condition in Italy where many individuals were attracted to the Jewish faith. If proselytes were won from among lower classes and noncitizens, Rome, manifesting its usual pragmatic approach to law enforcement, would look the other way. Even a few aristocratic Romans could be won over to Judaism without evoking overt retaliation. Nevertheless it was illegal, and this law could be invoked if the situation, as here, demanded it.

[22-24] Paul and Silas were stripped of their **garments**, beaten **with rods** (cf. 2 Cor. 11:25), and thrown into **prison**. Receiving charge for his prisoners was a serious part of the jailer's duty (cf. 12:19; 16:28).

Freedom from the Philippian Jail, 16:25-34. [25] Luke's picture of the Christian prisoners **praying and singing hymns to God** is another example of Paul's spiritual fortitude, a quality shining out on every page of his later letter, written from prison, to the believers at Philippi. Paul never let imprisonment stop him from witnessing and corresponding with his churches (24:24-27; 27:21ff.; 28:30; Eph. 6:20; Phil. 1:7, 13, 17; Col. 4:10, 18; Phile. 10; 2 Tim. 4:6-8).

²⁶and suddenly there was a great earthquake, so that the foundations of the prison were shaken; and immediately all the doors were opened and every one's fetters were unfastened. ²⁷When the jailer woke and saw that the prison doors were open, he drew his sword and was about to kill himself, supposing that the prisoners had escaped. ²⁸But Paul cried with a loud voice, "Do not harm yourself, for we are all here." ²⁹And he called for lights and rushed in, and trembling with fear he fell down before Paul and Silas, ³⁰and brought them out and said, "Men, what must I do to be saved?"

---

[26] Luke records here the third providential release of Christians from prison (cf. 5:19; 12:7-11), though in this case **all** prison **doors were opened and every one's fetters unfastened**. Historians of ancient literature and religion have rightly noticed the external similarity between this account and certain accounts of non-Christian religious leaders being miraculously freed from incarceration (Euripides, *Bacchae* 443ff., 586ff.; Ovid, *Metamorphosis* 3, 696f.; Artapanus in Eusebius, *Preparation of the Gospel* 9.27.23; Origen, *Against Celsus* 2.34).

[27] There was little forgiveness in the Roman Empire for a jailer who let his prisoners escape, for whatever reason (see 12:19). Paul, seeing that the jailer was preparing **to kill himself**, pleaded with him not to take his own life. None of the prisoners escaped.

[28] Paul's **loud voice** snatched the jailer back from his intended suicide.

[29] The shock of an earthquake . . . . . suicidal despair . . . . . a clamor for lights . . . . . trembling obeisance . . . . . and a cry for salvation. This scene is surely one of the most vivid and vibrant conversion accounts recorded by Luke.

[30] Whether the jailer had previously heard Paul proclaim the way of salvation (16:17) we do not know. And whatever this pagan jailer thought when he heard the term salvation, there is no doubt that the prior events convinced

[31] And they said, "Believe in the Lord Jesus, and you will be saved, you and your household." [32] And they spoke the word of the Lord to him and to all that were in his house. [33] And he took them the same hour of the night, and washed their wounds, and he was baptized at once, with all his family. [34] Then he brought them up into his house, and set food before them; and he rejoiced with all his household that he had believed in God.

[35] But when it was day, the magistrates sent the police, saying, "Let those men go." [36] And the jailer reported the words to Paul, saying, "The magistrates have sent to let you go; now therefore come out and go in peace."

---

him that Paul and Silas were spokesmen for the God who could help rescue him from the evil forces of his pagan environment.

[31] As quickly as the jailer asked, Paul answered, **Believe in the Lord Jesus.** Not only the jailer but also his **household** could be saved (for meaning of household see notes on 16:15).

[32] The **word of the Lord** was repeatedly the source of faith (cf. 4:29, 31; 8:25; 13:36; 14:25; 15:36).

[33] Luke uses the Greek *parachrēma* (**at once**) to emphasize the immediateness of the jailer's baptism (*parachrēma* occurs 18 times in the New Testament, 16 of these in Luke-Acts; cf. 3:7; 5:10; 12:23; 13:11; 16:26, 33). He and all of his family responded decisively.

[34] This short account ends with a beautiful picture of Christian hospitality (see notes on 16:15): wounds were cleansed, shelter given, food offered. Rejoicing (*agalliaō*) and joy characterized the believers (see note on 2:26). And now Paul, Silas, and the unnamed jailer were fellow believers, and all were freed from the chains which such a short time before had kept each of them in his own way in bondage.

Legal Vindication at Philippi, 16:35-40. [35, 36] The final episode at the Roman colony of Philippi is insightful in two

³⁷ **But Paul said to them, "They have beaten us publicly, uncondemned, men who are Roman citizens, and have thrown us into prison; and do they now cast us out secretly? No! let them come themselves and take us out."**

---

regards, namely, Paul's expedient use of his Roman citizenship (for fuller treatment of this see notes on 22:25) and Luke's use of this story in the overall themes of Acts. Luke does not record why the magistrates decided to **let those men go**. Perhaps they felt that Paul and Silas had learned their lesson. For whatever reason, the police (*rhabdouchos*) were sent to authorize their release. These police (mentioned only at 16:36, 38 in New Testament) were special officers, also known as lictors, assigned to magistrates. As a symbol of their police power they characteristically carried a bundle of sticks bound together with a red cord around an axe. The magistrates clearly intended to rid themselves of Paul by combining his release with his departure from town.

[37] Paul and his co-workers had "suffered and been shamefully treated at Philippi," as he was later to mention to the believers at Thessalonica (1 Thess. 2:2). Paul decided to demand an apology for their public beating, while **uncondemned**, and their imprisonment. There are probably several reasons that Paul chose, untypically, to stand and fight at Philippi, invoking his Roman citizenship as he did. It is extremely important to note that this was the first time that the source of Paul's sufferings was purely Gentile. When Paul was in "danger from my own people" (2 Cor. 11:26), he opted to tolerate Jewish hostility and live under their system of jurisprudence (a Jew to the Jews). However, in this situation he decided to use his Roman right to contend with Roman opponents.

Second, Paul may have felt, and judiciously so, that his claim that we are **men who are Roman citizens** would have greater impact in a Roman colony which prided itself on its conformity to Roman law and mores. And finally, there was little of the male-Jewish-synagogal base here so typically

³⁸ The police reported these words to the magistrates, and they were afraid when they heard that they were Roman citizens; ³⁹ so they came and apologized to them.

---

important in Paul's churches. This Jewish facet of Paul's churches helped protect the church from the law and society since Judaism was a legal religion in the Empire and the synagogue was a well-known part of society in almost all ancient cities. Without this base for the quasi-legal protection of the church, Paul may have decided to flex his legal muscle, as it were, and let the Romans know that the church would not take abuse, at least legally.

[38] Paul's emphatic "No!" (vs. 37) brought **the magistrates** to the Christians. They were afraid because it was illegal to subject **Roman citizens**, especially when uncondemned (*akatakritos*; cf. 22:25), to this kind of treatment (see notes on 22:25).

[39a] The climax of this story emerges when the municipal magistrates of this colony **apologized** to the Christians, who the day before had been in the stocks of the inner prison (16:24). The upshot, then, of this narrative is the legal vindication of Christianity and its leaders by the justice of Roman law. This theme abounds in Acts (see Introduction, part 1, pp. 15–17). That Paul's vindication made the magistrates look bad is inconsequential to Luke. In his commentary *The Acts of the Apostles,* Ernst Haenchen manifestly misunderstands this facet of Luke's theology. The story of 16:35-40 does not present "a problem very pressing for Luke" (p. 504). It is not Luke's ultimate intent with the stories involving Roman law to depict "the Roman authorities . . . as just, tolerant, even friendly to Christians" (p. 504). Roman officials, especially in the provinces, were often corrupt, injudicious, and pragmatic in their administration of justice. No self-respecting Roman would have even tried to defend provincial administrative practices. Luke's real intent is to show, even at the cost of confronting authorities, that Roman law (not officials) is just, tolerant,

And they took them out and asked them to leave the city.
⁴⁰So they went out of the prison, and visited Lydia; and when
they had seen the brethren, they exhorted them and departed.

¹Now when they had passed through Amphipolis and
Apollonia, they came to Thessalonica, where there was a
synagogue of the Jews. ²And Paul went in, as was his custom,
and for three weeks*ᵖ* he argued with them from the scriptures,
³explaining and proving that it was necessary for the Christ to
suffer and to rise from the dead, and saying, "This Jesus,
whom I proclaim to you, is the Christ."

ᵖOr sabbaths

---

and therefore friendly to Christians. This is the point of the
entire legal apologetic emphasis of early Christianity in
which Luke writes. And all we have here is an incident,
unlike that involving Gallio in 18:12-15, in which the
authorities chose to act against the justice of the Roman
legal system.

[39b, 40] Paul was still asked **to leave the city**. But before
complying with the request, he visited Lydia, his first
convert in Macedonia (for the significance of first converts
see 1 Cor. 16:15; Rom. 16:5). Following his practice of
encouraging and exhorting the men and women whom he
had converted, he departed. In all probability Luke stayed
behind and worked with the church there. This would
explain the fact that the "we" passages, which indicate
Luke's presence, end at this juncture and begin again in Acts
20:6, when Paul passes through Philippi again.

Paul and Silas at Thessalonica, 17:1-9

[1a] **Amphipolis and Apollonia** were smaller cities, a
day's journey apart on horseback, along the Via Egnatia.
Thessalonica, named after the sister of Alexander the Great,
was the provincial capital of Roman Macedonia and ranked
with Corinth and Ephesus in commercial importance.

[1b-3] Little is known from extrabiblical sources about
the Jewish community in Thessalonica, but in such an

important location it was surely prominent. As was Paul's **custom**, he immediately began to evangelize in the **synagogue** there (see notes on Acts 13:46). For **three weeks** (literally three sabbaths) Paul argued in the synagogue. The Greek term *dialegomai* (**argued**) did not carry the full weight and forcefulness of the English *argue*. This word appears here for the first time in Acts (17:2) and then again at 17:17 (mixed audience); 18:4 (synagogue); 18:19 (synagogue); 19:8 (synagogue); 19:9 (hall of Tyrannus); 20:7-9 (Christian assembly); 24:12 (mixed audience); and 24:25 (Felix and Drusilla). Luke's usage of *dialegomai* conveys not the picture of a quarrelsome attitude or irate apostle in the midst of debate or abusive attack on opponents. Rather, it depicts one setting forth religious or sermonic points in the hope of converting. In substance, this term *dialegomai* was synonymous with teaching and reasoning.

Paul's proclamation to the Thessalonians was in power and in the Holy Spirit and with full conviction (1 Thess. 1:5), but it never violated his basic posture of being gentle as a nurse with her children (1 Thess. 2:7; cf. 2 Tim. 2:24, 25).

Scriptures were the natural place from which Paul drew messianic proofs for his synagogue lesson. Luke was especially careful to point out both in his Gospel (note Luke 4:21; 18:31; 21:22; 22:37; 24:27, 32, 44, 45, statements unique to the third Gospel; see note on Acts 1:16) and Acts the importance of scripture fulfillment in Jesus' life and passion. Matthew is most often known for the frequent use of the prophecy-fulfillment motif because of his distinctively Jewish audience. Luke, however, also relied heavily upon this method. He stressed this to his Gentile readers to affirm the biblical truth (often forgotten by Gentiles) that Christianity cannot be understood apart from God's scheme of redemption begun with Israel and reflected in the Old Testament.

Explaining (*dianoigōn*) from the **scriptures** how **Jesus** was the **Christ** was an important facet of early Christian

⁴**And some of them were persuaded, and joined Paul and Silas; as did a great many of the devout Greeks and not a few of the leading women.**

---

preaching, teaching, and apologetics (see Acts 8:31). Unfortunately, centuries of Christian history dominated by an abysmal ignorance of the Old Testament has allowed many to believe, mistakenly, that a cursory reading of the Old Testament will immediately prove that Jesus is the Christ. However, Luke's use of this rare (in the Greek New Testament) word *dianoigō* proves otherwise. The word carries the basic idea of opening or revealing a truth which has been hidden, for whatever reason. One need only study Luke's use of the Greek word *dianoigō* in the Emmaus road encounter (Luke 24:13-35; esp. 24:32) or Jesus' farewell discourse (Luke 24:44-49; esp. 24:45) to appreciate the fact, expressed elsewhere in the New Testament (John 5:37-40; 1 Cor. 2:6-16; 2 Cor. 3:12–4:4), that the unaided reading of Scripture and human reasoning alone are not sufficient resources to acknowledge God's work in Christ. It is always God—never flesh and blood—who reveals that Jesus is the **Christ** (Matt. 16:17; 1 Cor. 12:3b; 2 Cor. 3:16).

Paul continued his teaching by **proving** that the true **Christ**, God's **Christ**, must (*dei*; cf. Acts 2:23) **suffer and rise from the dead.** Both **Jesus** and the twelve (Luke 9:22; 17:25; 24:7, 26, 44; Acts 3:18; 26:23; 1 Cor. 2:2; 15:3, 4; Gal. 3:1; 6:14; 1 Peter 1:11) taught that God's plan of redemption demanded a passion and resurrection. The goal of the apostle's plea was two-pronged: First, the **scriptures** taught that the **Christ** must **suffer**, die, and **rise** and, second, that this **Jesus** was the **Christ.**

[4] **Some** of the Jews who had listened to Paul for three sabbaths were **persuaded** by the teaching and consequently **joined Paul and Silas.** Luke's statement that a great many **Greeks** believed was intended to provide sharp contrast with the fact that only **some** of the Jews believed. This simple record of conversion results sheds light on an area of Paul's

⁵But the Jews were jealous, and taking some wicked fellows of the rabble, they gathered a crowd, set the city in an uproar, and attacked the house of Jason, seeking to bring them out to the people.

Thessalonian correspondence as well as on Luke's intent here. One could initially conclude that Paul's Thessalonian ministry was principally among and with Jews and lasted only a few weeks. We know, however, that Paul remained considerably longer there since he received two distinct contributions from the Philippian congregation while there (Phil. 4:16) and developed a great closeness with the believers at Thessalonica (1 Thess. 2:9-12, 17; 3:6).

It is manifest that Luke's primary purpose with this episode (17:1-9) was to contrast, once again, Gentile acceptance with Jewish rejection of the gospel message. Paul's letter to the congregation at Thessalonica confirms that the church there consisted primarily of Gentiles (1 Thess. 1:9; 2:14; also significant is the dearth of Old Testament quotations in 1 Thess.), although Aristarchus was probably a Jewish Christian from Thessalonica (Acts 20:4; 27:2; Col. 4:10, 11). Accordingly, Acts 17:4 may be viewed as the correct indicator of the racial composition of the church at Thessalonica.

In contrast to the devout women of high standing who opposed Paul and Barnabas at Antioch (14:50) **not a few of the leading women** at Thessalonica obeyed the gospel (17:4).

[5] The place of envy and jealousy (*zēloō*; cf. 5:17; 13:45) in the Jewish attacks on Christians has already been noted (on their propensity for riots see notes at 19:40, 41). The author's expression **some wicked fellows of the rabble** (*tōn agoraiōn*) connotes the city's troublemakers, hoodlums, loafers, and malcontents who loitered in the market area. A **crowd** was **gathered**, the city was thrown into a state of riotous confusion, and a mob rushed the **house** of a certain **Jason**. He may have been a Jew and he may have been a Christian, but neither is stated in the text. There is

⁶**And when they could not find them, they dragged Jason and some of the brethren before the city authorities, crying, "These men who have turned the world upside down have come here also, ⁷and Jason has received them; and they are all acting against the decrees of Caesar, saying that there is another king, Jesus."**

---

little doubt that he was associated by the mob with Paul, but beyond that we cannot know (Paul did have pagan friends, e.g., Asiarchs, in 19:31).

[6a] The juxtaposition of **Jason** with **some of the brethren** does not necessarily denote that he was not a believer (cf. Sosthenes at Corinth and Alexander at Ephesus in anti-Christian riots). The Greek word used by Luke which is loosely rendered **city authorities** is *politarchēs*. Archeological evidence further illuminates this municipal designation. This title has been preserved in approximately twenty inscriptions, principally from Macedonia, which show that each city had a number of these non-Roman magistrates. Thessalonica had five such officials in the first century. Luke has demonstrated once again that he was well informed on the particulars of Graeco-Roman municipalities and correct in his use of *politarchēs* for the **city** magistrates at Thessalonica.

[6b, 7] These verses report the charges brought against the believers. In the first place, they were accused of having **turned the world upside down**. The *oikoumenē* (civilized world) was an important concept in the mind of civil authorities in the period of the early Empire. The word *oikoumenē* connoted not only the *Pax* Romana, maintained by the emperor and his armies, but also brought to mind the universal influence of the Empire, both geographically and culturally. This unified *oikoumenē* was an accomplishment which has never again been achieved in the Mediterranean world. The joy of this blessing was still fresh in peoples' consciousness in Paul's day. The personal benefits derived from the *oikoumenē* were cherished by all, and no city or

individual would passively brook an anarchist sect which intended to turn **upside-down**, subvert, this *oikoumenē*. Examples of Roman pledges of allegiance from antiquity depict a zealous patriotism which would have been leery of Christian convictions.

We cannot be certain of the source of this misrepresentation of the church's message. One possible source is a Jewish, nationalistic perception of the Christian message of eschatology. F. F. Bruce judiciously observed thus: "It is clear from 1 and 2 Thessalonians that it [Paul's teaching] contained a prominent eschatological emphasis, which may have lent colour to the accusation" (*Acts*, p. 327).

The reader must also remember that just months prior to this episode the Emperor Claudius had expelled all the Jews and Jewish Christians from Rome itself for rioting and civil disobedience (see Acts 18:2). This, too, could easily have been the foundation of this charge against the disciples in Thessalonica, for both the account of the expulsion as well as those expelled traveled quickly toward Thessalonica along the Via Egnatia.

Jason is implicated in this because he **received** them as a host. Given the frenzied condition of the mob and their misconceptions about Paul's mission, Jason's act of hospitality was tantamount to harboring a fugitive or siding with seditious anarchists.

The second point in the charges was that of **acting against the decrees of Caesar**. Since the Caesar was both the titular and de facto keystone of imperial rule and government, the height of disloyalty was to support a rival contender who designed to usurp (typically through assassination) the position of the emperor. The charge that Jesus was a **king** (*basileus*) with imperial aspirations was also brought against the Lord himself (Luke 24:2). The title *basileus* in Jewish thought could refer to the Davidic king and God's Anointed (Luke 24:2). In the Roman context, however, it was synonymous with emperor (1 Peter 2:13, 17).

⁸And the people and the city authorities were disturbed when they heard this. ⁹And when they had taken security from Jason and the rest, they let them go.

¹⁰The brethren immediately sent Paul and Silas away by night to Beroea; and when they arrived they went into the Jewish synagogue. ¹¹Now these Jews were more noble than those in Thessalonica, for they received the word with all eagerness, examining the scriptures daily to see if these things were so.

---

[8] If the charges against the disciples had been true, **the people and city authorities** had every reason to be **disturbed** (deeply troubled). It could have been acutely detrimental to a city if it were guilty of condoning antigovernment agitators. Thessalonica was a free city (*urbs libera*). It had received this honor because it had sided with the victorious forces during the Roman Civil War. The privileges commensurate with this status were quite enjoyable and not to be jeopardized, particularly for the sake of (from a pagan perspective) a new religion with questionable tenets.

[9] **Jason and the rest** had to give **security** before they could be released. This was an established part of Roman jurisprudence and it was the politarchs' relatively mild method of securing tranquility in their city. The **security** or bond given must have required that Paul and Silas leave town immediately (and probably permanently).

Paul and Silas at Beroea, 17:10-15

[10a] The **brethren immediately sent Paul and Silas away by night**. When Paul later wrote to Thessalonica, he mentioned that he was prevented from returning there (1 Thess. 2:17, 18). This Satanic hindrance may be that he and Silas (though not Timothy, 1 Thess. 3:2) were *persona non grata* in Thessalonica, required by security never to return.

[10b, 11] Having **arrived** at Beroea, the apostles found a more receptive **synagogue** audience than at Thessalonica.

¹²**Many of them therefore believed, with not a few Greek women of high standing as well as men.**

Luke described them as **more noble** (*eugenesteroi*) **than those at Thessalonica.** Paul's message was the same as it had been in Thessalonica. But on this occasion it was planted in hearts characterized by **eagerness.** And this **eagerness** led to a **daily** (*kath hēmeran*; cf. 2:46; 3:2; 16:5; 17:17; 19:9; 1 Cor. 15:31; 2 Cor. 11:28) **examining** (*anakrinō*) of the **scriptures.** Those Beroean Jews were no supple yes-men of the apostles. Luke's term *anakrinō* suggests a serious inspection, examination, and discernment of Paul's teachings. Scripture was the acid test of the genuineness of Paul's instruction. John Calvin's commentary on this verse is noteworthy:

> They did only examine Paul's doctrine by the rule and square of the Scripture, even as gold is tried in the fire; for the Scripture is the true touchstone whereby all doctrines must be tried. . . . Therefore, let this remain as a most sure maxim, that no doctrine is worthy to be believed but that which we find to be grounded in the Scriptures.
>
> *(Acts of the Apostles*, vol. 2, p. 142)

[12] Several **greek women of high standing believed.** With previous Lukan references in mind (cf. 13:50; 16:13-15; 17:4) one begins to appreciate the religious autonomy of women in antiquity. Luke apparently believed that it was appropriate to emphasize the fact that **women** exercised independence in religious commitment (for the role of women in the Gospel of Luke, see vol. 4, part 1, pp. 15, 26f.). This Lukan posture sets him in sharp contrast with notable pagan male chauvinists such as Plutarch (*Advice to Bride and Groom* 140D), who believed that religious choice and activity were not desirable qualities in married women.

¹³But when the Jews of Thessalonica learned that the word of God was proclaimed by Paul at Beroea also, they came there too, stirring up and inciting the crowds. ¹⁴Then the brethren immediately sent Paul off on his way to the sea, but Silas and Timothy remained there. ¹⁵Those who conducted Paul brought him as far as Athens; and receiving a command for Silas and Timothy to come to him as soon as possible, they departed.

¹⁶Now while Paul was waiting for them at Athens, his spirit was provoked within him as he saw that the city was full of idols.

---

[13] Tenacity characterized the **Jews of Thessalonica** who came to Beroea to impede the **word of God** (cf. 9:1, 2; 14:19; 21:27). Fomented **crowds** (cf. 13:50; 14:5, 19; 17:5; 21:27) were once again the tool employed by the **Jews** to turn cities against the apostolic preaching.

[14, 15] Once more (cf. 17:10) Paul was ushered hastily out of the city by the **brethren**. Leaving the region of Macedonia and the three important churches established there—Philippi, Thessalonica, and Beroea—Paul journeyed to Achaia. **Timothy and Silas** were left behind at Beroea temporarily, but as soon as Paul arrived at **Athens** he commanded **for Silas and Timothy to come to him**. And although Timothy was quickly withdrawn from Beroea, he was still to play a significant part in Paul's further relationship with the churches of Macedonia (1 Thess. 1:1; 3:2, 6; 2 Thess. 1:1; Phil. 1:1; 2:19; Acts 18:5; 19:22).

Paul at Athens, 17:16-21

[16] Paul's brief evangelistic work at **Athens** was of more interest to Luke than to Paul himself. Except for a passing reference in one of Paul's letters (1 Thess. 3:1) the city of **Athens** is mentioned nowhere in the New Testament beyond Luke's description in Acts 17:16-34. The silence manifest in Paul's letters and the narrative given by Luke suggest that Athens yielded little fruit for the apostle's ministerial efforts

17 So he argued in the synagogue with the Jews and the devout persons, and in the market place every day with those who chanced to be there.

---

there. No representative from the Athenian church ever appears in the New Testament as a co-worker with Paul. Why then did Luke allot so much space to the account of Paul's work in Athens? In all probability, Luke was led to include this episode, unsuccessful as it was, in order to present to Theophilus (see notes at 1:1) and other Gentile readers the proclamation of the Good News in the cultural and philosophical center of the Graeco-Roman world. No stratum or facet of the inhabited world was beyond the range of the apostolic witness. Furthermore, it gave Luke the opportunity to preserve a record of a philosophical apology for the true knowledge of God and the Christian gospel.

With Paul's stringent Jewish upbringing and theological education against idolatry (Ex. 20:4; see notes on Acts 14:15) one would reasonably expect the apostle's **spirit** to be **provoked within him** on several occasions. Luke employed the forceful Greek word *paroxunō* to describe Paul's attitude toward the worship of **idols** (*paroxunō* is translated "irritable" in 1 Cor. 13:5 and "sharp contention" in Acts 15:39). It was noted by several authors of antiquity that **Athens** was indeed a city "full of idols." The Greek writer Pausanius commented that the Athenians worshiped the gods more than any other people and had more religion than any other city (*Description of Greece* 1.17.1; cf. Strabo, *Geography* 9.1.16; Josephus, *Against Apion* II.11).

[17] The apostle argued not only in the synagogue but also in the Athenian **market place** (*agora*, a description of which is detailed in Pausanius' literary travelogue of Attica). Marketplace preaching or teaching was commonplace in Graeco-Roman society. In both smaller towns and larger urban areas, the marketplaces were frequented by what has sometimes been called the philosophic missionary.

[18] Some also of the Epicurean and Stoic philosophers met him.

In a city so famous for its philosophic tradition and excellence there could be no more appropriate place to find the great apostle to all men than at the marketplace. In the manner of ancient philosophic missionaries and Christian street preachers the apostle Paul reached out to **those who chanced to be in the market.** It should be noted that this is one of the few recorded instances when Paul preached to such an unstructured and happenstance audience.

[18a] The **Epicurean** philosophy originated with the teachings of Epicurus (341–270 B.C.), who founded his school in Athens in about 306 B.C. His philosophical community, the first in antiquity to admit women, lived a simple and sober life. Epicurus, following the atomic theory of the philosopher Democritus, advocated an unyielding empiricism, a materialistic metaphysics to which even the gods were subject. Having assigned the gods and the rest of the sensible universe to a realm of arbitrarily moving atoms, Epicurus wanted to liberate mankind from the fear of gods, death, and religion. Along with this rather pessimistic metaphysics, Epicurus taught that the highest good was to avoid pain, discomfort, and trouble in this life and its human entanglements. Pleasure (defined as an absence of suffering, fears, and pain) was considered the highest good and the true goal of the philosophic journey. Opponents of Epicureanism twisted and slandered this quest for pleasure into a reputation for sensual pleasure. Thus the Epicureans were frequently, though falsely, accused of advocating a life of profligacy and concupiscence.

The **Stoic philosophers** and their teachings were very popular in the Graeco-Roman world. The founder of the influential stoic school, Zeno of Cyprus (335–263 B.C.), also studied in Athens and taught at the *Stoa Poikile* (Painted Hall). The Greek word *stoa* (meaning colonnade, porch, or hall) provided the name for the school. For the most part the Stoics were pantheists, with their god permeating all aspects

And some said, "What would this babbler say?" Others said, "He seems to be a preacher of foreign divinities"— because he preached Jesus and the resurrection.

---

of the universe. God was frequently designated as the eternal Logos (reason) or Spirit (*pneuma*) which guided the total direction and workings of the universe. While this cosmic Reason of the Stoics was conceived as having a real, independent existence, their descriptions of the gods were more often akin to personifications. Since cosmic Reason was God, rationality was offered as the only way to live in accordance with the revelation of Reason in the universe. Having jettisoned irrational impulses such as fear, compassion, pathos, pain, and emotions, personal ethics was then reduced to living in accordance with Reason revealed in nature. To live in harmony with nature meant to demonstrate a personal resignation in the face of the impersonal Reason of the universe. Passivity was the highest good, an attitude epitomized in a Stoic writer who explained that Providence leads those who are willing and drags those who are not.

Albeit the metaphysical base for the **Epicurean philosophers** (materialism) was quite different from that of the **Stoic philosophers** (materialistic pantheism), both schools of thought were incredulous at the Judaeo-Christian concept of God's transcendence over the cause-effect nexus of the natural order. Christian truth rested firmly on a supernaturalistic rather than naturalistic world view. This fundamental difference between the Christian and non-Christian metaphysical commitment, of course, had ramifications in other important areas such as ethics, revelation, and judgment.

[18b] Some of those who listened to Paul called him a **babbler** (*spermologos*). This graphic Greek word provides the reader with a glimpse into the eclectic world of ancient marketplace philosophy and preaching. The word literally means picking up of seeds as a bird might do. When applied

[19]And they took hold of him and brought him to the Areopagus, saying, "May we know what this new teaching is which you present? [20]For you bring some strange things to our ears; we wish to know therefore what these things mean."

---

to individuals, it denoted an individual who picked up, randomly as a scavenger bird or ragpicker, bits of popular wisdom, slick catchwords, slogans, and philosophical odds and ends and combined them into a hodgepodge message. This same term of abuse was used by the philosopher Dio Chrysostom of quack philosophers who spoke and harangued in the marketplaces of his day (see especially Wm. M. Ramsay, *St. Paul the Traveller and Roman Citizen*, pp. 242–244).

Others claimed that Paul preached **foreign divinities** (*xena daimonia*). For all the religious pluralism which existed in the Graeco-Roman world, there yet persisted the human fear of new things, especially new religions. And this fear also prevailed at Athens. Centuries earlier the urbane and enlightened citizens of classical Athens had indicted Socrates for importing strange divinities (Xenophon, *Memorabilia* 1.1.1; Plato, *Apology* 24b-c and *Euthypro* 3b. Luke was aware, as were knowledgeable readers of his day, that Paul's detracters were analogous to those who had condemned Socrates for similar reasons. Christian apologists of the early church frequently pointed out either directly or through allusions that Christian preachers were heirs of the best truth seekers of classical antiquity.

The conceptual chasm which separated Paul and his audience was manifest in the fact that they thought Paul was preaching two distinct **divinities**, one named **Jesus** and the other, **resurrection**. It is noteworthy that at least the Athenians correctly perceived that Paul's message centered upon **Jesus and resurrection** and were accurate in characterizing Paul as a preacher of **Jesus and resurrection** (cf. 1 Cor. 15:1-3).

[19, 20] These verses serve as a transition between

²¹Now all the Athenians and the foreigners who lived there spent their time in nothing except telling or hearing something new.

²²So Paul, standing in the middle of the Areopagus, said: "Men of Athens, I perceive that in every way you are very religious.

Paul's initial exchange with the Athenians and the presentation of his sermon. The reference to **new teaching** and **strange things** once again evoked in the reader's mind memories of respected Athenians who had similarly queried Socrates. When they brought Paul to the **Areopagus**, it was not for a formal trial but rather as a convenient occasion of the apostle to present his **new teaching** before the Council of the **Areopagus**. This council was assigned the task of looking into and discerning new philosophies and teachings which appeared in Athens.

[21] Luke observed that the **Athenians spent their time** in superficiality, always **telling or hearing something new**. This otherwise unlaudable penchant, mentioned by other ancient writers also, did afford Paul the opportunity to preach his gospel. Little did the Athenians realize just how **new** the message was that they were about to hear.

Paul's Speech before the Areopagus, 17:22-31

Introduction, 17:22-25. [22] Luke's wording that Paul stood **in the middle of the Areopagus** suggests the interpretation in the middle of the Council of the Areopagus rather than on the hill itself. Paul masked or subdued his previously provoked spirit (17:16), for he complimented the Athenians by commenting that they were **very religious** (*deisidaimōn*). Though *deisidaimōn* can mean either religious in a complimentary sense or superstitious in a pejorative sense, the apostle's use of it here conforms more to the former sense than to the latter. Pausanius also noted that the Athenians were more devout about religion than any other people (*Description of Greece* 1.24.3).

²³ **For as I passed along, and observed the objects of your worship, I found also an altar with this inscription, 'To an unknown god.' What therefore you worship as unknown, this I proclaim to you.**

[23a] The basis of Paul's statement about Athenian religiosity was the abundance of **objects of worship** (*sebasmata*; cf. 2 Thess. 2:4). Although these idols had infuriated the apostle earlier (17:16), he could observe that they were tokens of a religious spirit. Furthermore, as it was Paul's habit to "become all things to all men" (1 Cor. 9:22), it is not alarming for him to address the Athenians in such fashion.

[23b] It is not exceptional that archeologists have never unearthed this **altar** alluded to by Paul. However, the presence of such altars is well attested in ancient literature. And while Luke recorded only a single **altar** dedicated to a single **god**, we know that there were numerous altars dedicated to a plurality of unknown divinities. What is significant is that ancient non-Christian sources endorse Luke's accuracy here insofar as Athens was one of the cities best known for its altars to **unknown** gods. Haenchen's suggestion (*The Acts of the Apostles*, p. 521, note 2) that Luke's report about this **altar** to the **unknown god** was based on an ancient Greek travelogue-handbook, which Luke misinterpreted, is dubious.

Paul proclaimed to the Athenians that the unknown god (*agnostos theos*) whom they **worship as unknown** (*agnooomtes*) was about to become known to them. This homiletical introduction not only strengthened his rapport with his audience, but also obviated any later charges that he was importing new or strange divinities (cf. 17:18). This statement by Paul cut with a double edge, as it meant "that the heathen lived at one and the same time in a positive and negative relationship with the right God; they worship him and yet do not know him—they worship him indeed, but along with many other gods" (Haenchen, *The Acts of the Apostles*, p. 521; see esp. John 4:22).

²⁴**The God who made the world and everything in it, being Lord of heaven and earth, does not live in shrines made by man,** ²⁵**nor is he served by human hands, as though he needed anything, since he himself gives to all men life and breath and everything.**

[24a] As John Calvin noted on this verse, it was necessary for Paul to argue sequentially from the nature of God to the nature of worship, since the latter rests squarely upon the former (cf. John 4:24; Rom. 1:18ff.; Acts 14:15).

Although Paul never cited any Jewish Scripture in this gospel message, his doctrine of creation was rooted firmly in Jewish soil (see notes on Acts 14:15). Of course many ancient philosophies also acknowledged that Deity created the universe (e.g., Plato, *Sophist* 265b-d; *Statesman* 269d; *Timaeus* 29d-38c; *Laws* 10.886a).

[24b] Although not as cogent and forceful in style and content as Christian preachers, many ancient philosophic missionaries and intellectuals denounced the superstitious notion that Deity lived in man-made **shrines**. The Stoics and Cynics in particular ridiculed the naivete of the simple folk who believed, in a literalistic fashion, that temples and **shrines** were the abodes of divinity (e.g., Lucian, *Demonax* 27; *Lover of Lies* 20; Plutarch, *On Superstition* 167d). Consequently, even though Paul preached from his Jewish background, his message fell upon sympathetic ears in this audience of enlightened pagan philosophers.

[25] The God of Judaeo-Christian faith, unlike that of crass idolatrous superstition, **needed** nothing. Being Creator rather than part of the created (or manufactured) world, he is not **served by human hands.** Paul's thought here stems directly from the Jewish concept recorded in Psalm 50:9-12, where the writer argues that God does not need the sacrificial cult for his own well-being since he himself is creator of "the world, and all that is in it" (Ps. 50:12). Idols in pagan religions owed their very existence to an artisan's effort and priest's service (cf. Isa. 44:12-20; contrast 42:5).

[26] And he made from one every nation of men to live on all the face of the earth, having determined allotted periods and the boundaries of their habitation, [27] that they should seek God, in the hope that they might feel after him and find him.

God's Offspring, 17:26-28. [26] Earlier (17:24) Paul had affirmed God's lordship in heaven and on earth. He proceeds here to demonstrate the universal scope of this lordship on earth by reference to the creation of mankind. All races stem from **one** person (*ex henos*), i.e., Adam (cf. Rom. 5:12-21). Consequently, **every nation of men** owes its very existence to the creative power of this hitherto Unknown God. The apostle's doctrinal affirmation concerning creation eliminates any and all nationalistic, ethnocentric, and racist attitudes, ideologies, and theologies (cf. Rom. 3:29,30; Col. 3:10, 11). This fact gave Paul the ability to preach without attacking particular city or national deities which abounded in the Graeco-Roman world.

The expression **allotted periods** (*prostetagmenous kairous*) denoted the various seasons of the year. Once again Paul utilized a Jewish concept (Ps. 74:17b) to relate to a point of universal pagan experience, much as he had done in his Gentile sermon at Lystra (cf. 14:17, *kairous karpophous*). The background to the idiom **boundaries of their habitation** (*horothesias tēs katoikias*) was the Old Testament belief in the universal sovereignty of the Lord. The rise and fall of nations as well as national and international affairs of governments were all the arena of God's election and influence (Deut. 32:8; Ps. 74:17a).

[27a] In verses 26 and 27 Paul articulated two divine purposes of mankind. It was stated in Acts 17:26a that man was created; then in the Greek follow two infinitive clauses which give two purposes for this creation. The first infinitive clause in 17:26b states the purpose as "to live (*katoikein*) on all the face of the earth." The second Greek infinitive clause states that they should **seek** (*zētein*) **God.** These mandates and responsibilities of every man and

Yet he is not far from each one of us,

---

woman are, in fact, recorded in Genesis and rooted in the very creation of the human race. For as Genesis 1:26-31 so forcefully depicts, God's two pronouncements on mankind prior to the Fall were: men and women are spiritual creations of divine nature who bear God's likeness and image; and the earth and all of creation are under mankind's dominion and subjugation. Thus both foci of Paul's teaching regarding every nation descended from Adam, that they inhabit all the earth and that they **seek** fellowship with **God**, rested firmly on Jewish creation theology.

Since the Old Testament recorded principally God's dealing with an elect people, one finds there little of mankind's search for God. However, once the Jewish people were replanted by God in the diaspora, among peoples of all nations, this aspect of doctrine, namely, man's search for God, grew in significance and scope. This concept was tacitly affirmed in the early Hebrew belief that Yahweh was Lord of the nations, but only forcefully emerged once Judaism became a citizen, so to speak, of the Graeco-Roman world. Indicative of this growing interest is the Jewish work Wisdom of Solomon 13:1-9. Moreover, the dual phenomena of Godfearers and Jewish proselytes, products of the diaspora, are salient evidence that there were untold numbers of Graeco-Roman individuals who might **feel after** God and **find him.**

[27b] In this section Paul addressed the Athenians' relationship to God. For the creature in search of its creator the task is not impossible. God is **not far from each** person, not even those sometimes materialistic and supercilious Athenian philosophers. This nearness of God was not akin to the Stoic pantheism which rested upon the belief in God's immanence in all creation. Nor did Paul tie this concept of God's nearness to a Jewish view of God's presence in the temple or elective redemptive history. Rather Paul here articulated a distinctively Christian universalism which re-

²⁸ **for**

'In him we live and move and have our being';
as even some of your poets have said,
'For we are indeed his offspring.'

---

fused compromise to either an exclusivistic and sectarian Jewish understanding on the one hand or a pantheistic pagan view on the other hand.

[28] This verse contains two noncanonical citations, employed by Paul primarily to form a bridge between the Christian and non-Christian views of God. Since other noncanonical quotations are preserved in the Pauline letters (1 Cor. 15:33; Titus 1:12), it is not difficult to imagine that they would have also been appropriately used in a Christian sermon in Athens.

That Paul would speak in such pantheistic language as **in him we live and move and have our being** (*esmen*) has bothered some commentators. The conceptual background for this style of language cannot be located in the Old Testament, in spite of the attempts to find it there. Jewish people never spoke of living, moving, and being in Yahweh. However, Paul's frequent use of the expression "in Christ" (*en Christō*) may provide the solution to this enigmatic expression used before the Athenians. It has long been recognized that Paul frequently used similar and sometimes identical language to write about God and Christ (compare Col. 1:16, 17 with Rom. 11:36; cf. also 1 Cor. 8:6; Rom. 8:9-11; also Paul's use of Lord for both God and the Son of God). Accordingly, Paul's affirmation of the language of a pagan writer concerning God can be fitted into his own language concerning a Christian being in Christ.

The second literary citation (Aratus, *Phaenomena* 5; cf. Cleanthes, *Hymn to Zeus* 4) quoted by Paul proved to his audience that even their own thinkers agreed that all are indeed God's **offspring**. All came from one man Adam, and Adam was the son of God (Luke 3:38); therefore, the root of everyone's family tree was God himself (cf. Eph. 3:14, 15).

²⁹ **Being then God's offspring, we ought not to think that the Deity is like gold, or silver, or stone, a representation by the art and imagination of man.** ³⁰ **The times of ignorance God overlooked, but now he commands all men everywhere to repent,** ³¹ **because he has fixed a day on which he will judge the world in righteousness by a man whom he has appointed, and of this he has given assurance to all men by raising him from the dead."**

Call to Repentance, 17:29-31. [29] The upshot of Paul's teaching in verse 28 was not to assure his audience of a comfortable relationship with God or to excuse pagan practices, but to point up their culpability. Because men are **God's offspring**, they **ought not to think** in the categories of idolatrous religion, for idolatrous religion with its insistence that **Deity** (*to theion*) is a product of human **art and imagination** makes God inferior to **man** (cf. Pss. 115:4; 135:15; Isa. 44:9 and notes on Acts 14:15). How can the creator be made of elements such as **stone**, **silver**, or **gold**, which are inferior to man himself? Can the inferior create the superior? How can a spiritual entity—mankind—trace its lineage to a corruptible, perishable, handmade idol?

[30] Having proved the culpability of all mankind (17:29), the apostle next treated the **times of ignorance**. The Athenians could hardly have been offended at Paul's judgment of their **ignorance** (*agnoia*; cf. 3:17), since the very altar confessed an Unknown (*agnostos*) God. God's forbearance (*anochē*, Rom. 2:4; 3:26) and patience were important to Paul when he treated the theme of God's judgment. He expressed God's love for mankind with the term **overlooked** (*huperidōn*). However, his Athenian listeners could no longer hide behind God's previous overlooking their idolatry. They must live in the **now** (cf. Rom. 3:26; 16:26); responsibility had come to them since they had heard God's commands. Everyone, **everywhere** must **repent**.

[31] Stoic and Cynic popular philosophers of the Imperial Age preached the shortcomings of mankind and the

³²Now when they heard of the resurrection of the dead, some mocked; but others said, "We will hear you again about this."

---

need for individuals to repent. These philosophers, however, proclaimed nothing similar to the Judaeo-Christian concept of an eschatological judgment at the end of the Lord's redemptive history. None of the divine characters cast in the plays of Graeco-Roman mythology were transcendent, omnipotent, or holy enough to **judge the world in righteousness** (cf. Acts 10:42; Rom. 3:25, 26). The Pauline concept of a **fixed day** (cf. Rom. 2:5, 16; 1 Cor. 1:8; 3:13; 2 Cor. 1:14; Eph. 4:30; Phil. 1:6, 10; 2:16; 1 Thess. 5:2, 4; 2 Thess. 1:10; 2:2; 2 Tim. 1:12, 18; 4:8) arose uniquely from the Jewish concept of linear history wherein history moved, not in endless cycles but inexorably toward a final consummation.

Paul was unable to communicate the fulness of his Christology to these Athenian philosophers. He was, nevertheless, able to stress Jesus' divinity and place in God's plan with the term *horizō* (appoint). This Greek word is usually associated in the New Testament with persons, ideas, and events which hold a unique and divinely preordained place in God's revelation and economy (Luke 22:22; Acts 2:23; 10:42; 17:26; Rom. 1:4; Heb. 4:7). The **assurance** (*pistis*) of Jesus' role as **judge** of the living and the dead (10:42; 2 Tim. 4:1) was his own resurrection **from the dead**. This Christological perspective of the relationship between Jesus' resurrection and his divine status permeated the preaching and theology of the early church (Acts 2:36; 5:31; Rom. 1:4; 1 Thess. 1:10; Phil. 2:9).

Results of Paul's Sermon, 17:32-34

[32] Paul's preaching ended with a return to its starting point—Jesus and the **resurrection** (17:18). As with every audience, both Jewish and Gentile, the response to the preaching of Christ was mixed; some believed, others did

³³ So Paul went out from among them. ³⁴ But some men joined him and believed, among them Dionysius the Areopagite and a woman named Damaris and others with them.

¹ After this he left Athens and went to Corinth. ² And he found a Jew named Aquila, a native of Pontus, lately come from Italy with his wife Priscilla, because Claudius had commanded all the Jews to leave Rome.

---

not. Those Athenian philosophers who **mocked** did so because they, like the Jewish Sadducees, refused to believe in the possibility of a resurrection. The attitude of the typical well-educated Greek was epitomized by the statement preserved in Aeschylus' *Eumenides* (647f.), "Once a man is dead and the ground drinks up his blood, there is no resurrection" (*anastasis*, the same term used by Paul). Certain of those who had listened to Paul responded **we will hear you again.** We are not told of their ultimate response. One can only wonder whether they were truly stirred by Paul's preaching of this Unknown God or, like Felix (Acts 24:25), they practiced polite evasion.

[33, 34] A certain **Dionysius**, one of the Areopagites (a distinguished class of Athenians who made up the court of the Areopagus), **believed.** With this account Luke furnished another example of socially important individuals accepting the gospel (see Introduction, part 1, pp.15–17). Whether **Dionysius** became a bishop at Athens, as later tradition asserted, one can only speculate. We know nothing additional about the convert **Damaris** or the **others.**

Paul at Corinth, 18:1-17

Arrival at Corinth, 18:1-4. [1] Paul left a city famous for its contribution to Hellenistic culture and philosophy and **went to Corinth**, a city known for its vices and profligate mores, although admittedly **Corinth** had no monopoly among ancient seaports and urban areas on sexual abuses.

[2a] In Corinth Paul located two Jewish Christians, **Aquila** and his wife **Priscilla** (= Prisca), who were to be part

And he went to see them; [3] **and because he was of the same trade he stayed with them, and they worked, for by trade they were tentmakers.** [4] **And he argued in the synagogue every sabbath, and persuaded Jews and Greeks.**

---

of his ministry or in his memory for the remainder of his life (Rom. 16:3; 1 Cor. 16:19; 2 Tim. 4:19). These two had been forced to leave **Italy** in the general Jewish expulsion commanded by the Emperor **Claudius**. Members of various religious cults were driven from Rome and Italy from time to time in antiquity because of pernicious activity or sedition. Ancient secular writers (Suetonius, *Claudius* 25.4; Dio Cassius 60.6.6) mentioned an expulsion of Jews from Rome by the Emperor Claudius. While these sources cannot be totally harmonized, the traditional interpretation (following Suetonius) suggests that the cause for expulsion was the constant civil disturbances between Jews and Christians over the preaching of Christ. This view is supported again and again by episodes preserved in Acts. In all probability, then, the edict of **Claudius** mentioned by Luke is the imperial banishment issued about A.D. 49. This means that **Aquila** and **Priscilla** arrived in Corinth near the same time as Paul, A.D. 49–50.

[2b-4] Luke does not mention why Paul went to see these two, but it must have been because of their common faith. There were hundreds of Jews, both denizens and transients, in Corinth when Paul arrived, and no other explanation can be given for Paul's acquaintance with these two when he sought them out. This is the third time Luke has mentioned hosts of Paul (Lydia, Jason). The apostle's decision to live with these two was based on the fact that he had the **same trade**.

It is appropriate to note that Paul's trade was not exclusively tentmaking. The Greek term *skēnopoioi* originally meant **tentmakers**, but the meaning of the word changed through time so that first-century readers would have understood this to mean anyone who worked with

⁵**When Silas and Timothy arrived from Macedonia, Paul was occupied with preaching, testifying to the Jews that the Christ was Jesus. ⁶And when they opposed and reviled him, he shook out his garments and said to them, "Your blood be upon your heads! I am innocent. From now on I will go to the Gentiles."**

---

leather goods. In later correspondence with the Corinthian believers Paul reminded them that "we labor, working with our own hands" (1 Cor. 4:12). In fact, Paul frequently supported himself and his ministry by his own hard work, rarely receiving pay from the people to whom he ministered (Acts 20:34; 1 Cor. 9:1-18; 1 Thess. 2:9; 4:11; 2 Thess. 3:8; cf. also 2 Cor. 11:7-9; Phil. 4:15-17).

Turning to the Gentiles, 18:5-11. [5] When Silas and Timothy arrived from Macedonia, they surely refreshed Paul's spirits. He **was occupied with preaching**, and their presence must have eased the burdens which characterized Paul's Corinthian ministry. Timothy specifically carried good news of the faith and love of the Thessalonian Christians. Because of this report Paul was able to be comforted again and rekindle his spirits in spite of all the distress and affliction confronting him at Corinth (1 Thess. 3:6-10). Financial support from other Macedonian churches also freed him to spend more of his time directly pursuing his apostolic ministry (2 Cor. 11:8, 9).

[6] Corinth provided the second occasion for Paul's vociferous attack upon incorrigible Jews. Just as the Jews of Pisidian Antioch had **opposed and reviled** (*blasphēmeō*; cf. 13:45) Paul, so did those at Corinth. The Jewish blasphemy against the gospel received the same response as it did at Pisidian Antioch—a shaking of **garments** (cf. Matt. 10:14; Neh. 5:13) and a pronouncement of judgment. In the curse **your blood be on your heads**, the term **blood** means judgment of guilt (2 Sam. 1:16; Matt. 27:25).

Paul realized that the ultimate responsibility for a faith decision rested with the listeners; he was **innocent**

⁷And he left there and went to the house of a man named Titius⁹ Justus, a worshiper of God; his house was next door to the synagogue. ⁸Crispus, the ruler of the synagogue, believed in the Lord, together with all his household; and many of the Corinthians hearing Paul believed and were baptized. ⁹And the Lord said to Paul one night in a vision, "Do not be afraid, but speak and do not be silent;

⁹ Other early authorities read *Titus*

(*katharos*; cf. Gen. 24:8; Acts 20:26). Paul then turned to the **Gentiles** (see notes on Acts 13:46ff.; 15:15f.).

[7] Since the synagogue at Corinth, the ostensible place of scripture study, would not listen to the proclamation of Christ, Paul moved into the **house of a** certain **Titius Justus, a worshiper of God** (*sebomenos ton theon*; cf. Acts 16:14; 18:13). Presumably Paul used this house **next door to the synagogue** for his preaching. Aquila and Priscilla may have maintained a house church in Corinth as they did later in Asia (1 Cor. 16:19) and Rome (Rom. 16:3-5).

[8] **Crispus**, one of the rulers of the **synagogue** (*archisynagōgos*; cf. Mark 5:22, 35, 36, 38; Luke 8:49; 13:14; Acts 13:15; 18:17), was among the few converts personally baptized by Paul (1 Cor. 1:14) when he along with **all his household** (*oikos*; see note on 16:15) **believed**. The indefinite **many** (*polloi*) is used by Luke (cf. 4:4; 8:7, 25; 9:42; 13:43; 17:12) to describe the apostle's success. Little did Paul realize when these **Corinthians were baptized** that this would later be twisted into a divisive element in that congregation (1 Cor. 1:13-17).

[9] The **Lord** spoke to the apostle through a nighttime **vision** (see notes on 16:9). But there is a potential problem raised by this vision. Nothing in the Lukan narrative to this point would indicate reasons for Paul's uncertainty, fear, or ambivalence. In fact, the preceding text indicates only success. The later narratives likewise indicate success, since Paul is unharmed and vindicated in the presence of Gallio. It is only when the Corinthian correspondence is

¹⁰**for I am with you, and no man shall attack you to harm you; for I have many people in this city." **¹¹**And he stayed a year and six months, teaching the word of God among them.**

¹²**But when Gallio was proconsul of Achaia, the Jews made a united attack upon Paul and brought him before the tribunal,**

---

viewed as providing accurate supplementary information that Acts 18:9 is understandable. For there is no doubt on the basis of Paul's autobiographical reflections (1 Cor. 1:27; 2:3; 4:10; 2 Cor. 7:5; 10:10; 11:21, 30; 12:5, 9, 10; 13:9) that fear and weakness characterized his Corinthian ministry.

The tense of the imperative **Do not be afraid** (*mē phobou*) is present and perhaps communicates the idea of stop being **afraid**. Paul was neither the first nor the last spokesman of God who received special strength and confirmation from God to empower his ministry (cf. Ex. 4:1-17; Isa. 41:10; Jer.1:8; Acts 4:24-31; 27:21-25).

[10, 11] Two facts stand out in these verses. The most often noted fact is that God's promise to Paul that **no man shall attack you to harm you** stands adjacent to the reality of the fact that just two verses later (18:12) the Jews made a united attack upon Paul! Luke apparently understood the tenor of God's revelation in this context to mean that harm would not prevail over the apostle and impede his ministry. For a writer who understood this revelation too literally could hardly have juxtaposed this promise with the reality recorded in Acts 18:12. The second noteworthy fact is that the protection offered the apostle was exceptional and not for his own personal protection, but rather to assist in God's purposes (cf. Rom. 8:28b; 1 Cor. 4:9-13; 2 Cor. 11:23-28; Phil. 3:10; Col. 1:24, 25; Acts 9:16; 20:23; 21:13).

The reference to the **many people** (*laos*) whom God had in Corinth is an example of James' earlier statement about God taking a people from among the Gentiles (see notes on Acts 15:14-18).

Paul before Gallio, 18:12-17. [12] The proconsulship of

¹³saying, "This man is persuading men to worship God contrary to the law." ¹⁴But when Paul was about to open his mouth, Gallio said to the Jews, "If it were a matter of wrongdoing or vicious crime, I should have reason to bear with you, O Jews; ¹⁵but since it is a matter of questions about words and names and your own law, see to it yourselves; I refuse to be a judge of these things."

Gallio is one of the most important chronological benchmarks in the New Testament. **Gallio** is mentioned by several imperial writers and was a man of some importance as his election to the proconsulship of Achaia demonstrated. He was the brother of Seneca, the famous Stoic philosopher and tutor of Nero, and the uncle of the Latin writer Lucan. In addition to the Delphic inscription which is used to date his office in Corinth at A.D. 51–52 (and thereby furnish a chronologically datable point in Paul's life and ministry), he is also mentioned by Tacitus (*Annals* 12.8; 14.53; 15.73; 16:17), Pliny (*Natural History* 31.33), Dio Cassius (61. 20; 62. 25) and Seneca (*Moral Letters* 104.1).

[12b] The hostile **Jews** made a **united** (*homothumadon*; cf. Acts 1:14; 2:46; 4:24; 5:12; 7:57; 8:6; 12:20; 15:25; 19:29) **attack upon Paul** to bring him **before the tribunal** (*bēma*, cf. Matt. 27:19; John 19:13; Acts 12:21; 18:16, 17; 25:6, 10, 17; for God's and Christ's tribunal see Rom. 14:10; 2 Cor. 5:10).

[13] The Jewish charge against Paul on this occasion (cf. 17:6, 7; 21:20, 21, 28; 24:5, 6) was that Paul persuaded people to **worship God contrary to the law**. The **law** referred to here is not the Roman law, as in Acts 16:21, but the Jewish **law**.

[14] Even before **Paul** could refute the charge **Gallio** angrily reproached the Jews for bringing such an irrelevant issue before the judicial tribunal of the proconsul. This matter, according to Gallio, was patently unrelated to **wrongdoing** (*adikēma*; cf. 24:20).

[15] Having perceived that this was a matter regarding

¹⁶ **And he drove them from the tribunal.** ¹⁷ **And they all seized Sosthenes, the ruler of the synagogue, and beat him in front of the tribunal. But Gallio paid no attention to this.**

Jewish **words**, **names**, and **law**, the proconsul refused to apply civil or criminal jurisdiction to theological issues. Even though Gallio was the most powerful **judge** in the province, this type of case was not within his jurisdiction. Consequently, he ordered the Jews to **see to** the matter themselves (cf. Matt. 27:4, 24). Pilate had given the identical response to the Jewish mob who asked for Jesus' life (John 18:31).

[16] Apparently Gallio was an official of character and greater security, since unlike Pilate he refused to be intimidated by militant Jews. Rather than submitting to the Jewish pressure, Gallio **drove** the Jews from his presence. Thus this attempt to arrest the growth of the faith was stopped and, as the Lord had promised, Paul remained unharmed (18:10). This legal vindication before so important a Roman official must surely have encouraged Paul and the others. This episode also served Luke's apologetic interest concerning the legal respectability of the church (see Introduction, part 1, pp. 15–17).

[17] When Crispus converted to the faith (18:8), he was probably replaced as **ruler of the synagogue** by a certain **Sosthenes**. It surely would have been the synagogue adjacent to Justus' home which initiated the united attack against Paul. In all likelihood the new **ruler of the synagogue**, **Sosthenes**, would have directed this attack before the **tribunal**.

Who were the **all** who **seized Sosthenes**? Some ancient Greek manuscripts suggest that it was the Greeks who were favorable to Paul (18:6) and equally anti-Jewish in their attitudes toward the misanthropic Jewish leaders. Others suggest that it was Jews, angry over Sosthenes' mishandling of the litigation. We must await further data before a firm answer can be given.

**¹⁸After this Paul stayed many days longer, and then took
leave of the brethren and sailed for Syria, and with him
Priscilla and Aquila. At Cenchreae he cut his hair, for he had
a vow. ¹⁹And they came to Ephesus, and he left them there;
but he himself went into the synagogue and argued with the
Jews. ²⁰When they asked him to stay for a longer period, he
declined; ²¹but on taking leave of them he said, "I will return
to you if God wills," and he set sail from Ephesus.**

Return to Syria, 18:18-21

[18] With this legal victory behind him, Paul decided to
remain in Corinth for **many days longer. Priscilla and Aquila**,
"fellow workers in Christ Jesus, who risked their necks" for
Paul's life (Rom. 16:3, 4), became traveling companions of
Paul as far as Asia.

From **Cenchreae**, the important Corinthian port on the
Saronic Gulf, the trio sailed to Asia. Since the harbor town
of Cenchreae was situated approximately seven miles from
Corinth, it had its own congregation. The best known
leader of that congregation was Phoebe the deaconess
(Rom. 16:1).

Paul had been under a religious vow (*euchē*; cf. 21:23),
in all probability related to his ministry at Corinth. While the
apostle refused to require such of Gentiles, he as a Jewish
Christian kept up his observance of the Jewish ceremonial
law under various circumstances (cf. Acts 16:3; 20:16;
21:23-26; Gal. 5:11).

Scholarship is divided regarding the exact nature of this
vow. Since Paul cut his hair, this may be a Nazirite **vow**
(Num. 6:1-21; cf. Acts 21:23-26). Even though the Nazirite
vow required one to be in the temple at Jerusalem
(Num. 6:13-20), this was surely modified, as many other
things were, to accommodate the numerous Jews who lived
in the diaspora.

[19-21] Paul made a short stop in **Ephesus**, the capital of
Asia. Aquila and Priscilla were **left** in **Ephesus** and became
important leaders in the church there (1 Cor. 16:19).

²²When he had landed at Caesarea, he went up and greeted the church, and then went down to Antioch. ²³After spending some time there he departed and went from place to place through the region of Galatia and Phrygia, strengthening all the disciples.

During his brief stay in Ephesus Paul **argued with the Jews**, but obviously with cordiality since **they asked him** to remain **longer**. The apostle knew that God's plans for his life were larger and more complex than he himself could see. He had earlier been forbidden by God to preach the word in Asia (16:6). Having finally arrived in Asia, **he declined** the Jews' offer to continue his teaching there. His only comment to these hospitable Ephesian Jews, a rare breed in Paul's experience, was **"I will return if God wills."**

When the apostle sailed **from Ephesus**, he could hardly have imagined what a wide door the Lord would later open for his work in Ephesus (1 Cor. 16:8, 9), so wide that this city was to be the site of Paul's longest single ministry (Acts 19:10; 20:31).

PAUL'S THIRD JOURNEY, 18:22–21:25

Transition, 18:22, 23

[22, 23] Paul's ship **landed at Caesarea**, but his final destination was his home congregation at **Antioch**. Having concluded what is traditionally classified as his second missionary journey, Paul spent some time at Antioch. This gave him the opportunity both to rest and to report what God had done in his ministry (cf. 14:26-28).

Luke's narrative immediately pushes Paul into his third missionary journey. He began this final trip, just as he had others, by visiting congregations along the way in order to strengthen **the disciples** (see notes on 14:22; 15:41; 16:5). The reason Luke gave such an abbreviated account this time may be that he was pushing forward to report Paul's Ephesian ministry, the zenith of the apostle's work.

²⁴ Now a Jew named Apollos, a native of Alexandria, came to Ephesus. He was an eloquent man, well versed in the scriptures. ²⁵ He had been instructed in the way of the Lord; and being fervent in spirit, he spoke and taught accurately the things concerning Jesus, though he knew only the baptism of John.

Apollos, 18:24-28

[24] By preserving the historical information about the Alexandrian **Jew named Apollos** in **Ephesus**, Luke prepares the reader for the presence in Ephesus of a body of believers who knew only the baptism of John.

Apollos' significance was in the Corinthian church (1 Cor. 1:12; 3:4, 5, 6, 22; 4:6), though like Paul he worked in both the Corinthian and Ephesian churches (1 Cor.16:12). He is mentioned nowhere else in Acts.The intention of Luke in placing the two narratives (Acts 18:24-26 and 19:1-7) next to one another may have been to show the approach of Christians to believers in need of further instruction. Thus what Priscilla and Aquila did for Apollos (18:24-26) Paul will do for others like him in Ephesus (19:1-7).

Apollos was an **eloquent man** (*logios*; or perhaps meaning learned) who was **well versed** (*dunatos*, literally powerful) **in the scriptures.**

[25] Apollos had already been **instructed** (*katēchēmenos*; cf. Rom. 2:18; Gal. 6:6; Luke 1:4) **in the way of the Lord** (*tēn hodon tou kuriou*; cf. Matt. 3:3; Mark 1:3; Luke 1:76; 3:4; John 1:23). The use of the expression **way of the Lord** probably does not mean simply Christianity. While the Greek term *hodos*, translated **way** (Acts 9:2; 19:9, 23; 22:4; 24:14), refers to the church, the longer expression **way of the Lord** was always related to the preaching of John the Baptist. Consequently, being **instructed in the way of the Lord** was synonymous with speaking and teaching **accurately** (*akribōs*; cf. Luke 1:3; Acts 23:15, 20; 24:22) concerning the history of **Jesus** (Mark 5:27; Luke 24:19, 27; 23:11; 28:31).

²⁶**He began to speak boldly in the synagogue; but when Priscilla and Aquila heard him, they took him and expounded to him the way of God more accurately.** ²⁷**And when he wished to cross to Achaia, the brethren encouraged him, and wrote to the disciples to receive him. When he arrived, he greatly helped those who through grace had believed,** ²⁸**for he powerfully confuted the Jews in public, showing by the scriptures that the Christ was Jesus.**

¹**While Apollos was at Corinth, Paul passed through the upper country and came to Ephesus. There he found some disciples.**

Since Apollos **knew only the baptism of John** (cf. Matt. 3:11; Mark 1:4-8; Luke 3:3, 16; 7:29; 20:4; John 1:26, 31, 33; Acts 1:5, 22; 10:37; 13:24; 19:3, 4), he lacked that baptism by which the Spirit added one to the church (cf. 1 Cor. 12:13). Like the disciples discussed in Acts 19:1-7, he was in the rather unusual posture of being a post-Pentecost believer with pre-Pentecost instruction (cf. Acts 1:5).

[26] Aquila and Priscilla attended the Ephesian **synagogue**, probably continuing Paul's efforts there. When these two **heard** Apollos' accurate exposition, they took him aside and taught him **more accurately** (*akribesteron*) concerning **the way of God**. Noteworthy is Luke's irenic and complimentary description of this synagogue teacher who knew not the Savior's baptism.

[27, 28] Letters of recommendation were frequent in the early church (cf. 1 Cor. 16:3; 2 Cor. 3:1; Col. 4:10), and the believers at Ephesus wrote to their **brethren** in **Achaia** to **receive** Apollos. At Corinth **he powerfully confuted the Jews**. His learning in scripture (18:24) was put to good use there as he demonstrated **that the Christ was Jesus**.

Paul at Ephesus, 19:1-41

Disciples of John, 19:1-7. [1] After **Apollos** went to Achaia (18:27), **Paul** left Antioch and, going through Galatia

²And he said to them, "Did you receive the Holy Spirit when you believed?" And they said, "No, we have never even heard that there is a Holy Spirit." ³And he said, "Into what then were you baptized?" They said, "Into John's baptism." ⁴And Paul said, "John baptized with the baptism of repentance, telling the people to believe in the one who was to come after him, that is, Jesus."

---

and Phrygia (18:23), **came to Ephesus**. Luke's meaning of the word **disciples** (*mathētes*) here contributes to one's interpretation of this account. This word typically means Christians in the book of Acts, but some have argued that **some** (*tinas*) could refer to **disciples** of one other than Christ.

[2] Paul asked (probably because of some fact not transmitted to us by Luke) whether they had received **the Holy Spirit when** they **believed**. The correlation of receiving the **Spirit** with obedient faith was clearly Paul's way of describing conversion (Gal. 3:2; Eph. 1:13). Their response was that they had not **even heard** of the **Holy Spirit**. This translation, while possible, is highly misleading and improbable, for it implies that these men had never heard of the existence of the **Holy Spirit**. It surely transgresses the borders of reasonableness to believe that a group with even the slightest knowledge of John, baptism, and repentance (19:3, 4) would have **never heard that there** was **a Holy Spirit**. The Greek word *estin* lies behind the phrase **there is**. The same word, in the past tense, in John 7:39, also in conjunction with the advent of the Holy Spirit, is translated "had been given." All of the evidence (including textual variants) argues for this meaning in Acts 19:2. That is, these men had not **heard that** the **Holy Spirit** had been given.

[3, 4] The logic of Paul's response **into what then were you baptized** rested upon the fact that baptism and reception of the Spirit were integrally related (see notes on Acts 2:38). They could not have been properly **baptized** and yet be ignorant of the gift of the **Holy Spirit** (cf. Acts 2:38; 1 Cor. 12:13).

⁵ **On hearing this, they were baptized in the name of the Lord Jesus.** ⁶ **And when Paul had laid his hands upon them, the Holy Spirit came on them; and they spoke with tongues and prophesied.** ⁷ **There were about twelve of them in all.**

⁸ **And he entered the synagogue and for three months spoke boldly, arguing and pleading about the kingdom of God;**

The disciples acknowledged that they had received John's **baptism** rather than being **baptized** into Christ. Paul taught them that **John's** work was penultimate; his life and message pointed beyond itself to another (cf. 1:5; John 1:6-8, 15, 26; 3:30; 4:1; cf. Josephus, *Antiquities* XVIII.v.2).

[5-7] Having learned the true nature of the Baptist's ministry, they knew that loyalty to his message required that they look past him. Consequently, they were baptized with Christian baptism, namely, **in the name of the Lord Jesus.** As the story of evangelism in Samaria teaches (Acts 8:15-17), there was a reception of the Spirit beyond that received when **baptized in the name of the Lord Jesus.** There was on occasion the apostolic imposition of **hands** after baptism which imparted **tongues**, prophecy, and wonder-working powers (see the Simon incident, Acts 8:9-13, 17-24).

This was the third episode in Acts related to speaking **with tongues.** All three times this phenomenon related to a teaching on the **Holy Spirit** in the context of a significant incorporation of new groups into the church (2:4; 10:46; 19:5).

Separation from the Jews, 19:8-10. [8] Paul **entered** the Ephesian **synagogue** where months earlier he had preached and been asked to return (18:19-21). He spoke **boldly about the kingdom of God.** This idiom is used in Acts as a synonym for the Christian gospel (cf. 1:3; 8:12; 14:22; 19:8; 20:25; 28:23, 31). Although Paul's Ephesian ministry was lengthy (20:31), little good was accomplished in the synagogue there during these **three months.**

⁹ but when some were stubborn and disbelieved, speaking evil of the Way before the congregation, he withdrew from them, taking the disciples with him, and argued daily in the hall of Tyrannus.⁰ ¹⁰ This continued for two years, so that all the residents of Asia heard the word of the Lord, both Jews and Greeks.

¹¹ And God did extraordinary miracles by the hands of Paul, ¹² so that handkerchiefs or aprons were carried away from his body to the sick, and diseases left them and the evil spirits came out of them.

ᵣOther ancient authorities add *from the fifth hour to the tenth*

---

[9] A faction of the synagogue opposed Paul on account of their **stubborn** disbelief (cf. Rom. 2:5; Acts 7:51). The mind of the **congregation** (*plēthos*, as a technical term for religious communities; see also Acts 4:32; 6:2, 5; 15:12, 30; 25:24) was turned against the **Way** (*hē hodos*; see notes on Acts 9:2). Paul and the other disciples finally **withdrew** and relocated in the **hall of Tyrannus**.

[10] Paul argued (see notes on Acts 17:2) daily **for two years** in Tyrannus' hall. Even though this site came to be crucial in Paul's work at Ephesus, nothing is known either of this hall or of Tyrannus beyond what Luke informs us. Noteworthy is the fact that this non-Jewish base of operations served the apostle for the greater part of his stay at Ephesus. Moreover, this setting proved to be quite conducive to Paul's evangelistic thrust into **Asia** among **Jews and Greeks**. Most of **Asia** (e.g., Colossae, Laodicea, Smyrna) **heard the word of the Lord** directly or indirectly through the apostle's efforts in Ephesus (cf. 1 Cor. 16:9).

Sons of Sceva, 19:11-16. [11] These verses contain an account of **extraordinary** ancient Christian **miracles** and non-Christian magic. Wonders played a significant part in the ministry of Jesus (Acts 2:22; 10:38) and the apostles (see notes at 2:19).

[12a] **Handkerchiefs** and **aprons** were in this instance media for God's healing power. Numerous wonders re-

corded in the New Testament depended, as this one did, on the use of material objects and touch to bring the wonder to completion (cf. Luke 4:40; 5:13; 6:19; 8:54; 13:13; 22:51; John 9:6, 7; Acts 5:12, 15; 9:12; 14:3). Since Paul was the agent for God's performance of wonders, it was logical that these clothes would be impotent until coming into contact with the apostle's **body**.

The **sick** were the object of this wonder. The records of the ancient Mediterranean world indicate the existence of pagan cults and religions claiming to perform healing miracles. The sanctuaries of Asclepius (Pausanius, *Description of Greece* 2.27.3; plus numerous votive inscriptions), the autobiographical diary of a certain Aelius Aristides, scores of ancient papyri (e.g., *Oxyrhynchus Papyri* vol. 11, no. 1381), the works of Plutarch (esp. *On Superstition*), as well as the testimony of early Christian writers, prove that healing was a frequent concept in the religious thought of antiquity and thus naturally in the minds of the inhabitants of Ephesus. Epigraphical testimony shows that there were several priests and doctors of the healing cult of Asclepius at Ephesus.

Given the fact that this was one of the most frequent expectations and functions of ancient religions, the apostles forcefully and powerfully met the demands of their day with their God-given ability to heal the **sick**. Unlike some of their pagan contemporaries, they were not cure mongers or miracle hucksters, but they did, through God's power, meet the religious and evangelistic challenge of the day.

Luke's special interest in the word healing is seen both in his Gospel (esp. 4:18; 5:17; 6:18; 7:21; 8:47; 9:2, 42; 13:32; 14:4; 17:15; 22:51) and Acts (4:9; 5:15; 9:34; 28:8).

[12b] Both **diseases** (*nosos*; cf. Luke 4:40; 6:18; 7:21; 9:1) and **evil spirits** (*ta ponēra*; Luke 4:36; 6:18; 7:21; 8:29; 9:42; 11:24, 26; Acts 5:16; 8:7; 19:13, 15, 16) were expelled through God's power.

Though demons and **evil spirits** were rarely encountered in the Old Testament, there was a great awareness and

13 Then some of the itinerant Jewish exorcists undertook to pronounce the name of the Lord Jesus over those who had evil spirits, saying, "I adjure you by the Jesus whom Paul preaches."

---

sensitivity to their influence in later Judaism and by New Testament writers. The great majority of Graeco-Roman peoples believed in the operation of **evil spirits** in the sphere of sickness. Of course the writers of the New Testament did not believe that every sickness was a result of demon possession, or recuperation a direct intervention of God. On the other hand, the pagan understanding was so deeply rooted in a highly animistic and superstitious soil that almost anything could be a result of evil spirits (on the pagan view of deity see notes on Acts 14:11). Many of the better educated and levelheaded representatives of the Graeco-Roman world (e.g., Plutarch, Plotinus, Lucian, Plato, Cicero, Pliny, Galen, and the Hippocratic works) often complained that many had a penchant for relating every cure and sickness to the direct and immediate intervention of spirits and gods.

[13] Luke's record about the **Jewish exorcists** in his day is supported and confirmed by numerous ancient documents. In the first place, Jesus himself recognized the deeds of **Jewish exorcists** (Matt. 12:27; Luke 11:19; cf. Acts 13:6). Josephus (*Antiquities* VIII.ii.5), writings of the sectarian community at Qumran (*Genesis Apocryphon* of Cave 1; *Prayer of Nabonidus*), the Greek *Testament of Solomon* and Wisdom of Solomon (*7:17-20*), numerous magical papyri, as well as the evidence of the Christian writers Justin Martyr (*Dialogue with Trypho* 85.3), Irenaeus (*Against Heresies* II.vi.2), and Origen (*Against Celsus* IV.33), also noted the presence and workings of **Jewish exorcists**. Furthermore, in the imperial era Jews were often stock characters in Hellenistic magic (Juvenal, *Satires* 6. 540ff.; Augustine, *City of God* VI.11; Pliny, *Natural History* 31.18.24; cf. also Tobit 6:8, 17ff.; 8:3).

¹⁴**Seven sons of a Jewish high priest named Sceva were doing this.** ¹⁵**But the evil spirit answered them, "Jesus I know, and Paul I know; but who are you?"** ¹⁶**And the man in whom the evil spirit was leaped on them, mastered all of them, and overpowered them, so that they fled out of that house naked and wounded.**

These **itinerant exorcists** held a magical view of God's power. But rather than offering to purchase this power as Simon had done (Acts 8:18-20), they tried to steal it through the use of Jesus' **name**. The **name of the Lord Jesus** was a potent weapon in the apostolic arsenal. It was used in the performance of healings and confirmation of their preaching (see notes on Acts 13:12). The **name** of Jesus (see note on 2:21) could rightfully be utilized by one other than the twelve (cf. Mark 9:38, 39), but it was never intended to be used as a magical **name**, a hocus-pocus or abracadabra. It was biblical faith in his name that appropriated God's power for believers (Acts 3:16) and not the **name** per se. It was because the apostles had performed so many wonders in the **name** (i.e., under the authority) of Jesus (Acts 3:6, 16; 4:7, 10, 12, 30; 16:18) that these **Jewish** thaumaturgists misjudged (as some believers would, Matt. 7:22, 23) the power of **the name of Jesus** when it was not accompanied by an obedient faith.

[**14-16**] Luke identified these men as **sons of** the **Jewish high priest Sceva**, a person otherwise unknown in ancient records. The term **high priest** was used for other than the functioning high priest in Jerusalem, and priests were popularly associated with the power of exorcism. The demons protested at such attempts of exorcism by addressing the exorcists (cf. Mark 1:23; Matt. 8:28f.). In a somewhat comical scene Luke describes what happened to those who sought to exploit God's power reserved for his disciples. Actually these defeated exorcists escaped luckier than Bar-Jesus (13:11). They were attacked by the **evil spirit**, which sent them fleeing **naked and wounded**.

[17]And this became known to all residents of Ephesus, both Jews and Greeks; and fear fell upon them all; and the name of the Lord Jesus was extolled. [18]Many also of those who were now believers came, confessing and divulging their practices.

Magic, 19:17-20. **[17]** News of this overturning of Jewish magic spread quickly throughout the city. **Ephesus** was well known as a center of magic and the occult. What Athens was to classical philosophy and culture, what Corinth was to vice and profligacy, **Ephesus** was to the occult arts and thaumaturgy. An indication of the prominence and reputation of Ephesus in magic is found in the *Ephesian Letters* of antiquity. In ancient magic, multisyllable words and phrases such as abracadabra were a crucial ingredient in the working of spells. These syllabic gibberish sounds were collectively designated *Ephesian Letters*. In addition to the Jewish exorcists other miracle workers were known to have frequented **Ephesus** and performed wonders and exorcisms (Philostratus, *Life of Apollonius of Tyana* 4.10-11).

Fear (*phobos*) was a natural response to the manifestation of God's will and power, and Luke was especially interested in recording such responses to the display of the Lord's revelation (see notes at 2:43). **The name of Jesus was extolled** (*megaluno*; cf. Luke 1:46; Acts 5:13; 10:46) because of the power of this **name** (see notes on Acts 19:13). Many of those who **extolled the name of the Lord Jesus** were probably not Christians, as was sometimes the case in the early centuries of Christianity. One only need reflect upon the account of the adoration of Jesus by the pagan Magi (Matt. 2) to see another way in which non-Christian adoration and extolling could occur.

[18] A great number of **those who** became **believers** had skills and special expertise in the black arts of magic (on sorcery see Gal. 5:20; Rev. 9:21; 18:23; 21:8; 22:15). They both confessed and divulged their magical **practices** (*praxeis* = spells). The **divulging** of spells was tantamount to forsak-

¹⁹ **And a number of those who practiced magic arts brought their books together and burned them in the sight of all; and they counted the value of them and found it came to fifty thousand pieces of silver.** ²⁰ **So the word of the Lord grew and prevailed mightily.**

²¹ **Now after these events Paul resolved in the Spirit to pass through Macedonia and Achaia and go to Jerusalem, saying, "After I have been there, I must also see Rome."**

---

ing them, since their secrecy was a necessary ingredient in their supposed potency.

[19] Verse 18 narrated the response of believers who had kept ties with magic. This verse reports the response of nonbelieving magicians. Those who practiced **magic arts** (*perierga*) were so terrified that they collected **their books**— a key tool in their profession—and **burned them** (cf. James 2:19; Phil. 2:10).

Ancient literature contains records of other famous book burnings which demonstrated, in the sight of all, the repudiation of certain persuasions and beliefs (Livy 40.29; Suetonius, *Augustus* 31.1; Diogenes Laertius, *Lives of the Philosophers* 9.52; Lucian, *Alexander the False Prophet* 47; Tacitus, *Annals* 13:50; *Agricola* 2).

Fifty thousand pieces of silver was the worth of these **books** of magical prescriptions and occult spells. Because of their secret contents and supposed power to obtain cures, curses, love spells, horoscopes, etc., such books brought exorbitant prices.

[20] The expression **word of the Lord** is a synonym in Acts for the faith (6:7; 12:24; 13:49; 19:20; cf. also Luke 1:2 for eyewitnesses of the word) and for the content of what was preached (4:31; 6:2; 8:14, 25; 11:1; 13:5, 7, 44, 46, 48; 15:35, 36; 16:32; 17:13; 18:11; 19:10). The former meaning is assumed here, and this provides another example of Lukan summary statement (see notes on Acts 2:47).

Travel Plans, 19:21, 22. [21] Luke interrupted his narrative of Paul's ministry in Ephesus to preview Paul's itinerary

²² **And having sent into Macedonia two of his helpers, Timothy and Erastus, he himself stayed in Asia for a while.**

²³ **About that time there arose no little stir concerning the Way. ²⁴ For a man named Demetrius, a silversmith, who made silver shrines of Artemis, brought no little business to the craftsmen.**

---

through **Macedonia** (cf. 20:1; 1 Cor. 16:5; 2 Cor. 1:16). As in other instances in Paul's campaigns so here also his decision was **resolved in the Spirit** (cf. 16:6; 20:22; 21:4, 11). This report was the first revelation in Acts that Paul's face was to be set toward **Rome** via **Jerusalem**. Paul's sojourn in the region of **Jerusalem** will occupy most of the remainder of Acts (21:15–26:32), though his arrival in **Rome** is the ultimate object and focus of the last half of Acts. Once this destination had been announced, the remainder of Acts was structured around this goal. And the harbinger of Acts 19:21 was later confirmed by an appearance of the Lord (23:11), the charge of Festus (25:12), and an angel of God (27:24).

[**22**] Paul temporarily postponed his Macedonian visit and remained **in Asia for a while**. His letters confirm the sending of **Timothy** (1 Cor. 4:17; 16:10) **and Erastus** (2 Tim. 4:20; cf. Rom. 16:23) to Corinth.

Demetrius, 19:23-27. [**23**] Luke here depicts one of the most spectacular urban riots recorded in Acts. The activities and success of the **Way** (see notes on 9:2) produced **no little stir** (cf. 12:18) among the idolatrous artisans and devotees of Artemis in Ephesus. Luke clearly did not emphasize the enormity of this unrest, as pagan detractors might have, to depict the church as a fomenter of civil disobedience. Rather, he knew that a scene like this reflected the true ramifications and impact of the gospel upon its cultural surroundings.

[**24**] A certain **silversmith named Demetrius** was the antagonist in this public agitation against the believers in Ephesus. Unfortunately, nothing is known of this individual beyond what is preserved by Luke (attempts to identify this

²⁵**These he gathered together, with the workmen of like occupation, and said, "Men, you know that from this business we have our wealth.**

Demetrius with one mentioned in an Ephesian inscription are not persuasive). He was one of several **craftsmen** who manufactured **silver shrines of Artemis** as devotional items and relics. This reference to **silver shrines** has caused some (unwarranted) confusion and skepticism among ancient and modern commentators. Numerous ancient religions utilized miniature replicas of sanctuaries and **shrines** as a part of their devotional goods and regular equipment of their religiosity and piety (Petronius, *Satyricon* 29; Herodotus, *History* 2.63; Theophrastus, *Characters* 16.4; Diodorus Siculus 20.14.3). The reason that not one of these **silver shrines of Artemis** is extant is that they were made of a precious metal. Few silver items from antiquity have been preserved. This testifies to the value of the metal and its desirability, but not to the fact that such items never existed. Terra-cotta specimens of Artemis' **shrines** are extant.

[25] Demetrius **gathered together** those of **like** profession. There is abundant testimony from the Graeco-Roman world about the proliferation of trade guilds. The records are also clear in regard to the powerful influence that these guilds could and did exercise. From Asia Minor alone epigraphical sources mention guilds of silversmiths, goldsmiths, dyers, wool cleaners, cattlemen, fishermen, and bakers. And the fact that the efforts of Christian evangelism at Ephesus encountered such hostility from this labor guild "proves to the reader how genuinely the force of the Pauline mission makes itself felt, how deeply it shook the whole of heathenism" (Haenchen, *The Acts of the Apostles*, p. 578).

The prospect of financial loss is the catalyst for this riot and the source of the artisans' hostility. The **wealth** of these craftsmen was jeopardized because so many had ceased to buy the religious items manufactured by these men. Note that this is the second riot in Acts initiated by pagan rather

[26] And you see and hear that not only at Ephesus but almost throughout all Asia this Paul has persuaded and turned away a considerable company of people, saying that gods made with hands are not gods. [27] And there is danger not only that this trade of ours may come into disrepute but also that the temple of the great goddess Artemis may count for nothing, and that she may even be deposed from her magnificence, she whom all Asia and the world worship."

---

than Jewish hostility. And like the other Gentile riot (Acts 16:19-24) this one was also precipitated by the loss of revenue to businessmen rather than by the priests of a cult. Threats to the purse were frequently more unnerving and more cause of consternation than those to one's religion. The love of **wealth** was manifestly the root of the problem in Ephesus.

[26] Demetrius next argued that Paul **turned away a considerable company of** the **people** from the **gods**. This charge was tantamount to atheism. Paul's roots in Judaism as well as his knowledge of pagan philosophic arguments against idolatry (see notes on 17:24-29) made him especially adept in the battle against idolatry (cf. 1 Thess. 1:9). Consequently he **persuaded** multitudes to forsake the **gods made with hands**.

[27] To further stir the emotions and arouse the sympathies of his audience Demetrius invoked the sacred religion which was threatened. The **danger** was that this mushrooming Way, if left unchecked, would not only threaten their **trade**, but also **the temple of the great goddess Artemis**. The possibility that the goddess' **temple** might come to count for nothing was sufficient reason for these devotees and concerned citizens to feel trepidation. Ancient sources are replete with information on the importance of **Artemis** and her **temple** to the people of Ephesus. A brief description of Artemis' **temple**, the Artemisium, is appropriate at this juncture so that modern readers can see this episode with the eyes of Luke's contemporaries.

The Artemisium was situated approximately two kilometers outside the Roman city of Ephesus. The splendor and visual magnificence of the sanctuary were almost proverbial in ancient times. It was ranked as one of the seven wonders of antiquity (*Palantine Anthology* 9.58). Its size and wealth were unparalleled in the Graeco-Roman world (Pausanius, *Description of Greece* 7.5.4; 4.31.8), and it was the largest marble temple ever constructed. The importance of this sanctuary to ancient Ephesian and Asian civilization stemmed in part from its control of financial affairs. It served as a storage vault for wealthy aristocrats and commonwealths. Because of its sacredness and related invulnerability to attacks, it was considered to be the safest place to store large sums of money (Dio Chrysostom, *Orations* 31.54). Moreover, the goddess also maintained a financial empire of her own, managed by sacred ministers of her funds, which lent money, owned property, and collected sacred taxes (Strabo, *Geography* 14.1.26). A famous speaker of the second century noted that Ephesus and Artemis' temple were a source of refuge for Asia in time of financial need.

The temple was also involved in civic life. It sent its own representatives to Olympic games; it provided a place for the education of some children, having its own school located within the temple. Most civic and patriotic honors were awarded and inscribed there. The temple (much like the Jewish temple in Jerusalem) served as an asylum for certain types of social and political offenders. And finally, the temple served as the center of the **goddess Artemis'** religion, a place of prayer, sacrifice, sacred dedications, and revelations of the goddess through oracles.

It is clear then why the devotees of **Artemis** were ready to pitch battle with the followers of Christ over the fate of **the temple of the great goddess Artemis**. An Ephesian inscription (contemporary with Paul) conveys the pagan devotion to Artemis and her temple when it notes that the sanctuary of Artemis was the "ornament of the whole

²⁸When they heard this they were enraged, and cried out, "Great is Artemis of the Ephesians!" ²⁹So the city was filled with the confusion; and they rushed together into the theater, dragging with them Gaius and Aristarchus, Macedonians who were Paul's companions in travel.

---

province of Asia." Thus this cult was not just an integral part of society, but rather an integrating force of much of Ephesus' economic, religious, and cultural life. And the pagans there would understandably not brook serious threat from outside agitation or atheists.

Magnificence (*megaleiotētēs*, always a divine attribute; cf. Luke 9:43; 2 Peter 1:16) was Demetrius' claim for Artemis, and most of the ancient **world** agreed with him. He proudly claimed the spread of the goddess' cult throughout the Mediterranean **world**. Over thirty ancient locations have been identified. Her worship by the **world** is also preserved in ancient literature (Pausanius, *Description of Greece* 4.31.8) and epigraphical records (*British Museum Inscriptions*, vol. 3, no. 482B).

Great Artemis, 19:28-34. [28] The crowd was **enraged** (cf. Luke 4:28) when told the final consequences if the Way was not stopped. Their response was to chant **"Great is Artemis of the Ephesians!"** Central to the cult and mythology of the goddess was the fact that she was not merely the Greek **Artemis** (= Roman Diana) but that she was **Artemis of the Ephesians**. She was the patron goddess of the city, and it was her protectorate. The special concern of the Ephesians stemmed from the fact that the city was the international center and pilgrimage site for the cult (see notes on *neōkoros* in 19:35).

[29] The **city** was seized by **confusion**. This chanting, livid crowd found some of the leaders of the Way and, **dragging** these along behind **them, rushed into the theater**. This theater, still prominent among the ruins of the ancient city of Ephesus, seated approximately twenty-five thousand. Theaters in ancient society were multipurpose, serv-

³⁰Paul wished to go in among the crowd, but the disciples would not let him; ³¹some of the Asiarchs also, who were friends of his, sent to him and begged him not to venture into the theater. ³²Now some cried one thing, some another; for the assembly was in confusion, and most of them did not know why they had come together. ³³Some of the crowd prompted Alexander, whom the Jews had put forward. And Alexander motioned with his hand, wishing to make a defense to the people. ³⁴But when they recognized that he was a Jew, for about two hours they all with one voice cried out, "Great is Artemis of the Ephesians!"

---

ing as centers for performing arts as well as significant religious, political, and civic activities. Imperial edicts and new laws were read there. The city assembly (*ekklēsia*) regularly convened there. Prayers, sacrifices, and cultic festivals (especially those of the Ephesian Artemis) were conducted there. Since the charges against the Way had both civic and religious facets, the theater was the appropriate location to rally against the believers.

[30, 31] This was not the first time **Paul** had escaped the clutches of a howling mob (cf. 17:5-9). In this instance, though, Paul was convinced by the **disciples** (contrast 21:12-14) and the **Asiarchs** not **to venture into the theater**. This might well have meant Paul's death, and God had yet greater tasks for this apostle. He was not to die in Ephesus at the hands of a senseless mob. Noteworthy is Luke's reference to the **Asiarchs**. This fits into Luke's theme that leading citizens were friendly to the Christian faith (see Introduction, part 1, pp. 15–17). The office of Asiarch was usually held for one year, though renewable, by wealthy, well-educated, prominent citizens in each large urban area of Asia. Duties included the advancement and maintenance of the imperial cult. So close was the apostle to at least some of these **Asiarchs** that Luke called them his **friends** (*philoi*).

[32-34] So chaotic and precipitate had been the rush into the theater that **most** were unclear **why they had** assembled.

[35] And when the town clerk had quieted the crowd, he said, "Men of Ephesus, what man is there who does not know that the city of the Ephesians is temple keeper of the great Artemis, and of the sacred stone that fell from the sky?'

' The meaning of the Greek is uncertain

This was ostensibly a meeting of the city **assembly** (*ekklēsia*; cf. 19:41), the duly authorized meeting of the city government.

The ignorance which controlled this **assembly** was manifest in the action of some who **prompted Alexander**, a man **put forward** by **the Jews**. This Alexander wished **to make a defense to the** crowd. The **Jews** wished to extricate themselves from the guilt associated with the Jewish sect (as viewed by the Ephesians) led by Paul. Even though the Christians separated themselves from the synagogue at Ephesus (19:9) at an early date, the two—church and synagogue—lived and worked within the shadow of each other's activities.

The mob did not endure **Alexander** to speak **when they recognized that he was a Jew**; rather, they took up again their chant, **Great is Artemis of the Ephesians**.

Animosity toward Jews was prominent in Roman society, and this was the basis for the immediate rejection of **Alexander** by the Ephesian mob. Jews were accused of misanthropy in ancient times (Tacitus, *Histories* 5.5), and their aloofness and group loyalty were countered by the negative attitudes of pagans. Josephus confirms that there was considerable hostility between the Jews and non-Jews in Ephesus and Asia (*Antiquities* XVI. ii. 3,4; XIV. x. 11-19).

The Crowd Dismissed, 19:35-41. [35a] During the era of the early Roman Empire **the town clerk** (*grammateus*) was an official of exceptional influence in municipal government. He also served as representative of the city to imperial officials. Consequently, his treatment of followers of the Way in this public assembly was significant.

[36] **Seeing then that these things cannot be contradicted, you ought to be quiet and do nothing rash.** [37] **For you have brought these men here who are neither sacrilegious nor blasphemers of our goddess.**

[35b] The town clerk reminded the crowd that the **city was the temple keeper** (*neōkoros*) of **Artemis** as well as of **the sacred stone** from heaven. The Greek word for **temple keeper** was *neōkoros,* referring to a special privilege and responsibility which a city had toward specific deities or deity. Not all cities, not even all important ones, had this distinction. In fact, cities sometimes fought over the privilege, a privilege which meant they protected and maintained the cult of a divinity in return for the graciousness of the deity. Ephesians claimed that their city was the site of Artemis' nativity. And both inscriptional and numismatic evidence confirm that Ephesus was **temple keeper** for **Artemis** of Ephesus.

The second concept introduced by the clerk was that of the **sacred stone**. The Greek term *diopetēs* literally means fallen from heaven. This referred to the belief that the **sacred stone** (perhaps the first rock idol) of the religion fell from heaven, thus affirming the divine and transcendent origin of the religion; that is, it was not, as Paul claimed, made with human hands. Moreover, superstitious concepts and ancient cosmologies led to the belief that objects which **fell** from heaven were sacred and possessed apotropaic qualities (e.g., the meteorite venerated by the devotees of the Great Mother of Asia, Livy 29.10.4, 5).

[36] The force of the town clerk's argument was that since Ephesus' possession of the sacred stone and of the position of temple keeper **cannot be contradicted**, the Ephesians had no need to worry. In the mind of the town clerk this possession guaranteed the perpetuity and invulnerability of the religion of the goddess.

[37] Strange indeed was this response in the light of Paul's preaching (19:26). He declared that the Christians

[38] **If therefore Demetrius and the craftsmen with him have a complaint against any one, the courts are open, and there are proconsuls; let them bring charges against one another.** [39] **But if you seek anything further,' it shall be settled in the regular assembly.**

' Other ancient authorities read *about other matters*

---

were **neither sacrilegious nor blasphemers**. Commentators have suggested two solutions to this enigmatic assertion. The first is that this astute clerk, confident of Artemis' power, was principally interested in dispersing the mob (cf. 19:40):

> Like a trained advocate he ignores the real charge against the disciples, that of denying that images made with hands are gods, and declares that the men are neither templerobbers, nor blasphemers of the goddess.
>
> (McGarvey, *Commentary on Acts*, vol. 2, p. 167)

A second alternative is that Paul in fact had not reviled idols. The standard Jewish interpretation of Exodus 22:28a in New Testament times was that not even pagan gods were to be reviled (Josephus, *Antiquities* IV.viii.10; *Against Apion* 2.33; Ex. 22:28a, Greek).

[38] Having calmed the disorder, the city clerk placed the onus on **Demetrius** and his guild associates. It is important to observe that the charges and actions were brought against those of the Way by private citizens and not the government or municipal authorities. The enlightened jurisprudence of the Empire provided channels and methods for litigation. There were **open courts**, specific court days or sessions conducted under the aegis of the proper officials. **Proconsuls** are mentioned perhaps because of the seriousness of the charges. At certain periods there were more than one proconsul in the province of Asia.

[39] If Demetrius and his associates sought **anything further** or were reluctant (as well they should have been) to

[40]For we are in danger of being charged with rioting today, there being no cause that we can give to justify this commotion." [41]And when he had said this, he dismissed the assembly.

---

bring so flimsy a case before the proconsul, they ought to bring it before **the regular assembly** (*hē ennomos ekklēsia*). According to John Chrysostom, the regular assembly met three times each month. The shrewdness of the town clerk is again evident in his refusal to defer to this angry crowd.

[40, 41] Rioting was a constant thorn in the flesh in ancient municipal life. Numerous civil disturbances erupted in the wake of Christian growth (*thorubeō*, 17:5; 20:10; *plēthos*, 14:4; 21:36; 25:24; *thorubos*, 20:1; 21:34; 24:18; *stasis*, 15:2; 19:40; 23:7, 10; 24:5; *anastatoō*, 17:6; 21:38; *ochlus*, 16:22; 17:13; 21:27, 35; *sustrophē*, 19:40; 23:12). Roman imperial officials kept a constant eye on all organizations, especially specious labor unions (Pliny, *Letters* 10.34). Dio Chrysostom sternly warned residents of his Asian hometown that nothing which takes place in cities escapes the proconsul's eye (*Orations* 46.14). Consequently, the Ephesian town clerk rightly warned that they might be **charged with rioting**. If not curbed, this riot could have led to the disbanding of the silversmiths' guild, punishment of responsible municipal officials, and, in extreme cases, the forfeiture by Ephesus of its status as a free city. Roman history recorded more than one example of a city losing its privileges for similar injudicious actions.

The clerk could find no crimes committed by the believers so **he dismissed the assembly** (*ekklēsia*). The biased accusations of Demetrius could not justify such a **commotion** in the Romans' eyes. What a victory for the Way! The believers were exonerated by the leading municipal official (for this theme see part 1, pp. 15–17). Moreover, the pagan opponents of the church, rather than the church, were censured for engendering civil disturbances and endangering the venerable *Pax* Romana.

105

¹**After the uproar ceased, Paul sent for the disciples and having exhorted them took leave of them and departed for Macedonia.** ²**When he had gone through these parts and had given them much encouragement, he came to Greece.** ³**There he spent three months, and when a plot was made against him by the Jews as he was about to set sail for Syria, he determined to return through Macedonia.** ⁴**Sopater of Beroea, the son of Pyrrhus, accompanied him; and of the Thessalonians, Aristarchus and Secundus; and Gaius of Derbe, and Timothy; and the Asians, Tychicus and Trophimus.**

Paul in Greece, 20:1-6

[1] As was the apostle's custom, he had fellowship with and exhorted (*parakaleō*; see notes on 14:22) the **disciples** before he left them, never to see many of them again (cf. 20:16, 17). Paul set out for **Macedonia**, intending to rendezvous with Titus (2 Cor. 2:12, 13; 7:5-8).

[2] The journey through **these parts** may have followed the apostle's earlier steps (cf. Acts 16:11, 12). This sojourn in Macedonia may have given this evangelist the opportunity to preach the gospel of Christ as far as Illyricum (Rom. 15:19).

[3] During Paul's **three months** in Greece, he not only continued arrangements for the Jerusalem collection, but probably wrote his letter to the Romans. When knowledge of yet another Jewish **plot** to kill him (cf. Acts 9:24; 20:19; 23:16, 20; 25:3; 2 Cor. 11:26) surfaced, he altered his plans. Instead of going by sea from Cenchreae to **Syria** (cf. 18:18) he turned north and traveled into **Macedonia** again, eventually setting sail from Philippi (20:5).

[4] Luke here includes the names of several in Paul's company. These were representatives with credentials (1 Cor. 16:3, 4) to deliver the Jerusalem collection. **Sopater**, **Aristarchus, and Secundus** were the delegates from the Macedonian congregations. **Gaius and Timothy** were from Galatia, while the **Asians** included **Tychicus and Trophimus**.

⁵These went on and were waiting for us at Troas, ⁶but we
sailed away from Philippi after the days of Unleavened Bread,
and in five days we came to them at Troas, where we stayed
for seven days.

⁷On the first day of the week, when we were gathered
together to break bread, Paul talked with them, intending to
depart on the morrow; and he prolonged his speech until
midnight. ⁸There were many lights in the upper chamber
where we were gathered. ⁹And a young man named Eutychus
was sitting in the window. He sank into a deep sleep as Paul
talked still longer; and being overcome by sleep, he fell down
from the third story and was taken up dead. ¹⁰But Paul went
down and bent over him, and embracing him said, "Do not be
alarmed, for his life is in him."

[5, 6] These delegates to Jerusalem went on, probably
carrying the contribution (1 Cor. 16:3), and **were waiting for**
Paul and Luke at **Troas**. At this juncture is the second of
three **we** passages which encompasses 20:6–21:18. The
author of Acts apparently joined the apostle at **Philippi**,
precisely where the first **we** passage indicates Paul left him
(16:17). Waiting until **after the days of Unleavened Bread**
(cf. 1 Cor. 16:8), they sailed for **Troas**. There they remained
for seven days (cf. 21:4; 28:14).

Paul at Troas, 20:7-12

[7] The **first day of the week** (cf. Matt. 28:1; Mark 16:2;
Luke 24:1; John 20:1, 19; 1 Cor. 16:2) was the most important occasion for assembly in the early church. They had
assembled **to break bread** (cf. 2:42, 46; 20:11; 27:35; Luke
24:30, 35), which meant either eating a meal or having the
Lord's supper, or both. (The first interpretation is taken by
Beginnings of Christianity, vol. 4, pp. 255, 256; the second
by McGarvey, vol. 2, pp. 179, 180 and Haenchen, p. 584;
the third by F. F. Bruce, p. 408).

[8-10] Luke preserves here a curious vignette, to which
he had been an eyewitness. The Christians had assembled in

¹¹And when Paul had gone up and had broken bread and eaten, he conversed with them a long while, until daybreak, and so departed. ¹²And they took the lad away alive, and were not a little comforted.

¹³But going ahead to the ship, we set sail for Assos, intending to take Paul aboard there; for so he had arranged, intending himself to go by land. ¹⁴And when he met us at Assos, we took him on board and came to Mitylene. ¹⁵And sailing from there we came the following day opposite Chios; the next day we touched at Samos; and" the day after that we came to Miletus. ¹⁶For Paul had decided to sail past Ephesus, so that he might not have to spend time in Asia; for he was hastening to be at Jerusalem, if possible, on the day of Pentecost.

"Other ancient authorities add *after remaining at Trogyllium*

---

an **upper chamber** (1:13; 9:37, 39; cf. Mark 14:15; Luke 22:12), specifically on the **third story**. **A young man named Eutychus sank into a deep sleep.** When finally overtaken by **sleep**, he **fell** out of the window in which he sat. He was **taken up dead** because of the distance of the fall, but **Paul**, after **embracing him**, said **"Do not be alarmed, for his life** [*psuchē*] **is in him"** (cf. Matt. 9:24; Mark 5:39 [if the youth was in fact dead]; cf. 1 Kings 17:21).

[11, 12] **Paul** went back up to the upper chamber, having been interrupted by this accident. Consequently it was the next morning (Monday morning according to F. F. Bruce, p. 409; McGarvey, pp. 181, 182 reckons otherwise) when they were able, after the delay caused by Euthychus' injury, to break bread (*klasas ton arton*; cf. 20:7) and eat their food (*geusamenos*). During the next several hours, **until daybreak**, Paul conversed with them.

Travel to Ephesus, 20:13-16

[13-16] Luke and the others left Troas setting **sail for Assos**. **Paul** walked the distance, reflecting either his displeasure at the thought of sailing the rough, open water

¹⁷And from Miletus he sent to Ephesus and called to him the elders of the church. ¹⁸And when they came to him, he said to them:

"You yourselves know how I lived among you all the time from the first day that I set foot in Asia, ¹⁹serving the Lord with all humility and with tears and with trials which befell me through the plots of the Jews; ²⁰how I did not shrink from declaring to you anything that was profitable, and teaching you in public and from house to house, ²¹testifying both to Jews and to Greeks of repentance to God and of faith in our Lord Jesus Christ.

---

between Troas and **Assos** or the need for some time to himself perhaps to contemplate the rough waters which lay ahead of him in Jerusalem. Having rendezvoused with the others at **Assos**, he boarded the ship for **Miletus**. Paul was so conscious of the Lord's mandate to go to **Jerusalem** that he even forsook the opportunity to visit the churches in **Ephesus** and **Asia**. Paul's desire to be **at Jerusalem on the day of Pentecost** revealed both his habit of keeping Jewish customs (cf. Acts 18:18; 21:26) and his desire to visit **Jerusalem** at a time propitious for contact with as many Jewish Christians as possible.

Paul's Farewell Address, 20:17-35

Summary of Ministry, 20:17-24. [17] The mention of **elders** (*presbuteroi*; cf. Acts 11:30; 14:23; 15:2, 4, 6, 22, 23; 16:4; 21:18; 1 Tim. 5:1, 2, 17, 19; Titus 1:5; James 5:14; 1 Peter 5:1, 2) **of the church** at **Ephesus** shows that this was a normative office in congregations associated with Paul's work (Acts 14:23).

[18-21] This section gives supplementary information for a balanced picture of Paul's Ephesian ministry by having him remind the elders of his credentials (1 Cor. 4:9-16; 9:1, 2; 2 Cor. 3:1-3, 7-12; 1 Thess. 1:5, 6; 2:9, 10). **Humility** (*tapeinophrosune* and cognates, 2 Cor. 10:1; 11:7; Eph. 4:2; Phil. 2:3, 8; 4:12; Col. 3:12; 1 Peter 3:8) and **tears** (20:31;

²²**And now, behold, I am going to Jerusalem, bound in the Spirit, not knowing what shall befall me there;** ²³**except that the Holy Spirit testifies to me in every city that imprisonment and afflictions await me.** ²⁴**But I do not account my life of any value nor as precious to myself, if only I may accomplish my course and the ministry which I received from the Lord Jesus, to testify to the gospel of the grace of God.**

---

2 Cor. 2:4; 2 Tim. 1:4) could not be circumvented by this great apostle in his **serving the Lord**. Portraits such as these provide a balance to the more triumphal apostolic results in other parts of Acts (e.g., 19:10-20, 23-41; cf. 1 Cor. 15:32; 16:19; 2 Cor. 1:8-10). **Plots of** hostile **Jews** always plagued the apostle's ministry (cf. Rom. 15:31; 1 Thess. 2:14-16; and note on Acts 20:3). **Public teaching** included the marketplace as well as the Ephesian hall of Tyrannus (19:9). The expression **house to house** (*kat' oikous*) assumed the presence and constant use of house churches (cf. *kat' oikon* in Acts 2:46; 5:42; 8:3; 1 Cor. 16:19; Col. 4:15; Phile. 2) for church **teaching**. J. W. McGarvey observed that "in the true apostolic method of evangelizing a community, and of edifying a congregation, earnest work from house to house was on par with that in the pulpit" (*Commentary on Acts*, vol. 2, p. 187).

[22-24] This part of Paul's exhortation was a harbinger for the remainder of his ministry. As a willing slave **bound in the** Holy **Spirit** rather than by iron manacles, the apostle was led **to Jerusalem** (19:21). The **Holy Spirit** was a constant channel of God's will and revelation to Paul (cf. 13:2, 3; 16:6-8; 19:21; 21:4, 11). **Imprisonment** was a regular part of the apostle's life, and as a convict he continued to perform his ministry. Paul could boast of his "far more imprisonments" (2 Cor. 11:23); the apostle's incarcerations are mentioned in Acts (16:23-40; 20:23; 23:18, 29, 35; 25:14, 27; 26:29, 31; 27:1, 42; 28:16, 17), 2 Corinthians (6:5), Ephesians (3:1; 4:1), Philippians (1:7, 13, 14, 17), Colossians (4:18), 2 Timothy (1:8; 2:9), and Philemon (1, 9, 10, 13).

²⁵ **And now, behold, I know that all you among whom I have gone preaching the kingdom will see my face no more.**

Afflictions (*thlipsis* 14:22; 20:23; Rom. 5:3; 8:35; 12:12; 2 Cor. 1:4, 8; 2:4; 4:17; 6:4; 7:4; 8:2, 13; Eph. 3:13; Phil. 1:17; 4:14; Col. 1:24; 1 Thess. 1:6; 3:3, 7; 2 Thess. 1:4, 6; *thlibō* 2 Cor. 1:6; 4:8; 7:5; 1 Thess. 3:4; 2 Thess. 1:6, 7; 1 Tim. 5:10; see notes on Acts 9:16 and 14:22) so characterized the apostle's life that he could say "I bear on my body the marks of Jesus" (Gal. 3:17; cf. 1 Cor. 4:9-13; 2 Cor. 6:4-10; 11:23-29).

Paul set no **value** on his own **life**. Following the Savior's teaching "For whoever loses his life for my sake and the gospel's will save it" (Mark 8:35; Matt. 16:25; Luke 9:24), Paul did not **account** his **life as precious** to himself.

This soldier of the cross epitomized a single-minded obedience toward **the ministry** (cf. 2 Cor. 4:1; 6:3; Col. 4:17; 2 Tim. 4:5) which he **received from the Lord Jesus** (see notes on Acts 9:15, 16). Paul's description of his ministry as a **course** (*dromos*) is well known from his letters, where he frequently used imagery and metaphors from the struggles of the stadium and gymnasium to accentuate the rigors and efforts of the disciplined Christian life (1 Cor. 9:24-27; Gal. 2:2; 5:7; Phil. 2:17; 3:13, 14; 2 Tim. 2:5; 4:7, 8; cf. Acts 13:25). It is worthy of mention that the Greek noun *euaggelion* (**gospel**) occurs only twice in Acts (here and 15:7) and never in Luke's Gospel.

Charge to Elders, 20:25-31. [25] This is the second section of this address which begins **And now** (cf. 20:22, 32). **Preaching the kingdom** (see notes on 1:3 in part 1) is an idiom in Luke (8:1; 9:2) and Acts (28:31). This verse reflects Paul's intention never to return to his Aegean mission field (cf. 20:38). At this point he intended to shift his emphasis to Rome and the West, particularly Spain (Acts 19:21; Rom. 1:15; 15:23-28). If Paul did in fact later visit Asia (1 Tim. 1:3), this would furnish another example of change in Paul's itinerary (see notes at Acts 16:6-8).

²⁶**Therefore I testify to you this day that I am innocent of the blood of all of you,** ²⁷**for I did not shrink from declaring to you the whole counsel of God.** ²⁸**Take heed to yourselves and to all the flock, in which the Holy Spirit has made you overseers, to care for the church of God**ᵛ **which he obtained with the blood of his own Son.**ʷ

ᵛ Other ancient authorities read *of the Lord*

ʷ Greek *with the blood of his Own* or *with his own blood*

[26, 27] The apostle was **innocent of the blood** (cf. 18:6) of the Ephesian elders. The idiom **shrink from declaring** (cf. 20:20) attested the apostle's boldness as well as integrity in fulfillment of his commission. Unlike Cephas (Gal. 2:12), who in one instance shrank back, Paul consistently maintained his integrity (cf. the tenor of Heb. 10:38, 39, where this same Greek verb *hupostello* and its noun occur). The expression **counsel of God** is used only by Luke (Luke 7:30; Acts 2:23; 13:36; 20:27) among the authors of the New Testament (cf. Eph. 1:11; Heb. 6:17 for a similar concept). **The whole counsel of God** is synonymous with "anything that was profitable" in Acts 20:20.

[28] The injunctive statement **take heed to yourselves and to all the flock** forebodes the heresies which were to strike the Ephesian Bishopric (for similar uses of *prosecho*, see Matt. 7:15; 10:17; Luke 17:3; 20:46; 21:34; Acts 5:35). A similar admonition is preserved in 1 Timothy 4:16, where Timothy is warned: "Take heed to yourself and to your teaching; hold to that, for by so doing you will save both yourself and your hearers." Leaders can hardly watch after those under their charge if they cannot first **take heed** introspectively.

The continual interest and debate concerning the office of elder justify a brief note at this point. In the first place, this portion of scripture demonstrates beyond question that in the early church the designations elders (*presbuteroi,* 20:17), **overseers** (*episkopoi,* 20:28; identical word is rendered bishops in Phil. 1:1; 1 Tim. 3:2; Titus 1:7 and guardian in 1 Peter 2:25) and shepherds (*poimainō*, 20:28; 1 Peter 5:2; *poimnion*, 20:28, 29; 1Peter 5:2, 3) were synonymous. Just as the Greek terms *episkopos* (1 Peter 2:25) and *apostolos* (Heb. 3:1) refer to both Christ and selected individuals, so does the term *shepherd* (*poimēn*, Christ in John 10:2-16; Heb. 13:20; 1 Peter 2:25; individuals in Eph. 4:11). The important antecedents for this dual use of the word *shepherd* are in the Old Testament (e.g., Ezek. 34; Jer. 3:15; 23:1-4).

The second portion of this scripture reveals the relationship between the elders and the **Holy Spirit**. Foremost is the fact that the duty or office is a selection or gift of God's **Spirit**. Paul taught here that the **overseers** were **made** such by the **Holy Spirit** (though the dynamics of such selection are not detailed). The quality of this ruling position as a divine gift is likewise taught in Paul's letters. Most notable is Ephesians 4:11, where the apostle listed pastors (*poimēn*) among the gifts of Christ's grace. The Greek term *kubernēsis* used in 1 Corinthians 12:28 ("administrators") meant someone who steered or piloted a ship or governed people. This task was clearly assumed by more than one person (plural used in 1 Cor. 12:28) and it was clearly a *charisma* of God's Spirit (1 Cor. 12). Since the description of piloting or governing is closely aligned with what can be known from other teaching about the role of elders, many rightly interpret this also as a reference to elders.

Thus the apostle Paul definitely taught that the office and role of bishops were controlled by the **Holy Spirit** and not the converse. Unlike postapostolic ecclesiastical developments, the writers of the New Testament did not believe that the office of bishop controlled the **Holy Spirit** (or the word or baptism and the Lord's supper) or afforded the holder of such office any exalted status. **To care** (*poimainein*) for **the flock** was the job description, and this task clearly did not remove one from the requirement of self-examination (20:28) or the real possibility of apostasy (20:30).

²⁹**I know that after my departure fierce wolves will come in among you, not sparing the flock;** ³⁰**and from among your own selves will arise men speaking perverse things, to draw away the disciples after them.**

The expression **church of God**, found only here in Acts, is a favorite Pauline expression for the saved (1 Cor. 1:2; 10:32; 11:16, 22; 15:9; 2 Cor. 1:1; Gal. 1:13; 1 Thess. 2:14; 2 Thess. 1:4; 1 Tim. 3:5, 15). The apostle's expression **which he obtained with the blood of his own Son** is couched in terms and allusions from the Old Testament. The Greek verb *peripoieō*, translated **obtained** (noun form is *peripoiēsis*) is reminiscent of Isaiah 43:21 (Greek) "my people whom I have preserved (*peripoieō*) to tell forth my praises." A kindred thought is preserved in 1 Peter 2:9, "you are a . . . people for his possession (*peripoiēsis*)." The doctrine of the blood atonement is likewise rooted in Jewish experience. The price of obtaining **the church of God** was nothing less than the **blood of his own Son** (cf. Rom. 3:25; 5:9; 1 Cor. 11:25; Eph. 1:7; 2:13; Col. 1:20; Heb. 9–10; 1 Peter 1:2, 19; 1 John 1:7; Rev. 1:5; 5:9).

[29, 30] The apostle Paul was not one to ignore the turbulent times which the Ephesian church faced. And all indications from the Pastoral Epistles (1 Tim. 1:3), Revelation (2:2-6), and later church history confirm Paul's prophecy. The figure of **fierce wolves not sparing the flock** is a poignant description of a heresy's devastating effect on the church (cf. Matt. 7:15; John 10:12). Such individuals, whether they came from outside or arose from the bishopric, were not tolerated by Paul. For as he had earlier instructed the Corinthians, those who destroy the church of God will, in turn, be destroyed by God (1 Cor. 3:17).

Even the eldership of the Ephesian church would spawn men **speaking perverse things** (cf. 1 Tim. 4:1). In one sense, the history of God's people has been a history of apostasy (cf. Stephen's speech) and worthless leaders. The Old Testament frequently employed imagery of worthless shep-

³¹**Therefore be alert, remembering that for three years I did not cease night or day to admonish every one with tears.** ³²**And now I commend you to God and to the word of his grace, which is able to build you up and to give you the inheritance among all those who are sanctified.**

---

herds to teach about faithless leaders (cf. hireling in John 10:12,13). Illustrative of the background of Paul's stern imagery is a judgment oracle (one of many) in Zechariah 11:15-17, which should be heeded by every generation of God's leaders.

The **perverse things** were probably incipient Gnosticism, a mixture of Christianity with other beliefs. The schismatic and sectarian spirit which would **draw away the disciples** was itself heretical (Rom. 16:17-20; 3 John 9, 10).

[31] Paul concluded this section with the admonition **be alert**. He mentioned once again (cf. 20:20) the constancy of his admonitions to them. The **three years** noted here establishes the fact that as far as can be known Paul's longest single ministry was in the city of Ephesus.

Missionary's Example, 20:32-35. [32] As Paul was about to bid farewell to this bishopric and faced with the fact that the infant church, as always, stood at the fork in the road, one path leading to life and the other to destruction, he said all that he could say. In the final analysis, all Paul could do was **commend** (*paratithēmi*, Acts 14:23; 1 Peter 4:19; cf. Rom. 14:14; 16:25; Eph. 3:20; Phil. 4:19; Col. 1:11; 1 Thess. 3:13; 5:24; 2 Tim. 1:12; Jude 24) them to the care of **God and** his **word of grace.** Even in the situation of impending apostasy, Paul refused to jettison **the word of his grace.** To be sure one must understand the grace of God in truth (Col. 1:6), but no circumstance or abuse of grace (cf. Rom. 3:8; 5:20–6:2; Gal. 5:13; 1 Peter 2:16; 2 Peter 2:19) convinced Paul to deny, in his words, "the ministry which I received from the Lord Jesus, to testify to the gospel of the grace of God" (Acts 20:24). The power **to build up** (*oikodomeō*) is nothing less than this **word of his grace.**

³³I coveted no one's silver or gold or apparel. ³⁴You yourselves know that these hands ministered to my necessities, and to those who were with me. ³⁵In all things I have shown you that by so toiling one must help the weak, remembering the words of the Lord Jesus, how he said, 'It is more blessed to give than to receive.' "

Love builds up (1 Cor. 8:1), and running throughout Paul's doctrine is the belief that the knowledge of the **grace** of God is the prime mover for Christian works (Titus 3:4-8; Eph. 2:8-10; 1 Cor. 15:10).

[33-35] One might have anticipated Paul's concluding this address with the benediction of 20:32. However, he continued with a teaching about Christian eleemosynary activities. The elders must likewise concern themselves with charity. Paul argued first from the example of his own toil in life (see 1 Cor. 4:16; 11:1, 2; 2 Thess. 3:7-9). Paul performed his duty and **coveted no one's silver or gold or apparel**. All things in his life demonstrated the necessity of helping **the weak**, that is, those unable adequately to provide for themselves (cf. Gal. 2:10). As he so clearly taught elsewhere, the disciple is to work in order not just to keep busy and look to his own needs, but especially "so that he may be able to give to those in need" (Eph. 4:28).

More important than imitating Paul's life was **remembering the words of the Lord Jesus**. While Paul rarely quoted material from the **Lord** (e.g., 1 Cor. 7:10, 12, 25; 11:23-25; 1 Tim. 5:18), he surely knew more than his letters mention. This particular saying of Jesus "**It is more blessed to give than to receive**," never found in the canonical Gospels, is classified along with other such examples as *agrapha* (i.e., not recorded). However, it clearly portrays the self-sacrifice, altruism, and servanthood which dominated Jesus' words and deeds (e.g., Luke 6:38).

This sermon, the longest address to believers in Acts, provides a pattern for the church when deprived of apostolic presence.

116

³⁶And when he had spoken thus, he knelt down and prayed with them all. ³⁷And they all wept and embraced Paul and kissed him, ³⁸sorrowing most of all because of the word he had spoken, that they should see his face no more. And they brought him to the ship.

¹And when we had parted from them and set sail, we came by a straight course to Cos, and the next day to Rhodes, and from there to Patara.ˣ ²And having found a ship crossing to Phoenicia, we went aboard, and set sail. ³When we had come in sight of Cyprus, leaving it on the left we sailed to Syria, and landed at Tyre; for there the ship was to unload its cargo.

ˣOther ancient authorities add *and Myra*

An Emotional Parting, 20:36-38

[36-38] These verses record what must be one of the most emotive scenes of the Bible, taking its place alongside the reunion of Joseph with his family, David's dirge for Saul and Jonathan written in the Book of Jashar, and Jesus' lament over Jerusalem. So constrained by emotion, weeping, and sighs too deep for words, **Paul knelt** to pray, illustrating yet again that his indomitable spirit was rooted in a transcendent power (e.g., Rom. 8:18-39; 2 Cor. 1:3-11; 4:7–5:5; Phil. 4:4-7, 10-13). The Greek idiom for kneeling is found in Acts 7:60; 9:40; 20:36; 21:5; Mark 15:19; and Luke 22:41 (cf. Luke 5:8; Eph. 3:14; Phil. 2:10). So deep was the anguish of these bishops that **they all wept, embraced** (lit. fell on his neck) and **kissed** Paul (for this practice, see Gen. 33:4; 45:14; 46:29; Luke 15:20; cf. Rom. 16:16; 1 Cor. 16:20; 2 Cor. 13:12; 1 Thess. 5:26; 1 Peter 5:14).

The thought **that they should see** Paul's **face no more** was a great source of sorrow for these men. Farewells must finally end, so **they brought** Paul **to the ship** bound for Syria.

Travel to Phoenicia, 21:1-6

[1-3] These few verses narrate an uneventful voyage from Asia to **Tyre** with a midcourse change of ships at

⁴And having sought out the disciples, we stayed there for seven days. Through the Spirit they told Paul not to go on to Jerusalem. ⁵And when our days there were ended, we departed and went on our journey; and they all, with wives and children, brought us on our way till we were outside the city; and kneeling down on the beach we prayed and bade one another farewell. ⁶Then we went on board the ship, and they returned home.

⁷When we had finished the voyage from Tyre, we arrived at Ptolemais; and we greeted the brethren and stayed with them for one day. ⁸On the morrow we departed and came to Caesarea; and we entered the house of Philip the evangelist, who was one of the seven, and stayed with him. ⁹And he had four unmarried daughters, who prophesied.

Patara. The latter half of the journey was apparently completed on a larger **ship** which needed not to stay close to shore. Since Paul was anxious about an early arrival in Jerusalem (cf. Acts 20:16), he decided to travel in open seas, with **Cyprus on the left**, thus removing the necessity of making numerous stops along the southern shore of Turkey. **At Tyre,** Paul, Luke, and the others disembarked.

[4-6] They remained at Tyre **seven days** (cf. Acts 20:6) and chose to spend that time with **disciples** whom they had **sought out**. These **disciples** told Paul **not to go on to Jerusalem**. That these **disciples** were enjoined thus by the Holy **Spirit** is unlikely since Paul's mission to Jerusalem was initiated by the **Spirit** (19:21). What transpired at **Tyre** is parallel to the later episode at Caesarea (21:11-14). The Holy **Spirit** predicted Paul's Jerusalem sufferings (cf. 20:23) and the disciples, unable to bear this thought, begged Paul to resist the Spirit's leading (see notes on Acts 21:14). This **farewell**, as at Miletus, ended in **kneeling** prayer.

Visit at Caesarea, 21:7-14

[7-9] The next stopover was the Roman colony **Ptolemais**, known in Old Testament times as Acco (Judges

¹⁰**While we were staying for some days, a prophet named Agabus came down from Judea. ¹¹And coming to us he took Paul's girdle and bound his own feet and hands, and said, "Thus says the Holy Spirit, 'So shall the Jews at Jerusalem bind the man who owns this girdle and deliver him into the hands of the Gentiles.' "**

1:31) but later renamed for Ptolemy II (285–246 B.C.). Having stayed there **one day**, the party traveled on to **Caesarea**, perhaps by ship. There they remained with the probable founder of the Christian community at **Caesarea** (Acts 8:40), **Philip**. It was appropriate for Luke to designate him the **evangelist**, since this was partly what Luke knew his work to have been (cf. Acts 8:12, 35, 40). The other way **Philip** (not the apostle, Matt. 10:3; Mark 3:18; John 1:43-48; Acts 1:13) was known to Luke's readers **was** as **one of the seven** (Acts 6:3; apparently it was only apostles and not evangelists who should not serve tables).

Philip's **four unmarried** (*parthenoi*) **daughters** were prophetesses. Women (both married and unmarried) who prophesied were well known in Old Testament writings and were usually women of stature, for example, Miriam (Ex. 15:20), Deborah (Judges 4:4), Huldah (key figure of authority in Josiah's reform, 2 Kings 22:14; 2 Chron. 34:22), Noadiah (Neh. 6:14), and the nameless prophetess of Isaiah 8:3. Luke also knew of the widowed prophetess Anna (Luke 2:36-38), who spoke of Jesus in the temple precinct. It is unclear whether Luke intended by this reference to bring to mind the Joel prophecy (Joel 2:28-32) cited on Pentecost, which authorized prophetesses in the early church (Acts 2:17).

[10, 11] Paul and his entourage remained there **for some days**. The Judean **prophet Agabus** (cf. 11:27f.) met them there and delivered a passion prediction (cf. Mark 10:33) for Paul, as he himself had earlier foretold (20:23). Agabus' prophecy, following a practice in the Old Testament, consisted of a symbolic gesture as well as verbal explanation of

¹²When we heard this, we and the people there begged him
not to go up to Jerusalem. ¹³Then Paul answered, "What are
you doing, weeping and breaking my heart? For I am ready
not only to be imprisoned but even to die at Jerusalem for the
name of the Lord Jesus." ¹⁴And when he would not be
persuaded, we ceased and said, "The will of the Lord be
done."

---

the prophetic gesture (cf. 1 Kings 11:29ff.; 22:11;
Isa. 20:2ff.; Jer. 13:1ff.; Ezek. 4:1ff.). Agabus' gesture was
taking **Paul's girdle** and binding **his own feet and hands**. This
symbolic action pointed to Paul's being bound in chains of
captivity (cf. John 21:18). **Thus the Holy Spirit** interpreted
this to portend that Paul would be delivered **into the hands**
(cf. Matt. 17:22; 26:45; Mark 9:31; 14:41; Luke 9:44; 24:7;
Acts 2:23) **of the Gentiles**, a fact that was to occur presently
(21:33).

[12] The Christians protested and **begged** Paul **not to go
up to Jerusalem**. Their weeping (cf. Acts 9:39; 20:37) was
almost more than Paul could endure.

[13] The translation **breaking** rests upon a rare Greek
term *sunthruptō*, which signified crushing or breaking something to pieces. Paul's response **What are you doing?**
(cf. Acts 14:15; Mark 11:5) was meant as a rebuke. His
co-workers and fellow believers were at the point of
weakening Paul's resolution (caught in the throes of seeing
God's will over against their own). But the apostle recon-
firmed the way of obedience by pledging his readiness (not
to be confused with the morbid eagerness manifested in the
martyrdom of later Christians) **not only to be imprisoned** (see
notes on Acts 20:23) **but even to die at Jerusalem**. Though it
was not in the Lord's plan, Paul may well have anticipated,
especially after Agabus' prophecy, his death in **Jerusalem**.

[14] When it finally became clear to Luke (**we**) and the
rest that Paul could not be deterred, they **ceased**, in resignation, and said, **"The will of the Lord be done"** (see
Matt. 6:10; 26:42; Luke 22:42; *Martyrdom of Polycarp 7.1*).

¹⁵After these days we made ready and went up to
Jerusalem. ¹⁶And some of the disciples from Caesarea went
with us, bringing us to the house of Mnason of Cyprus, an
early disciple, with whom we should lodge.

¹⁷When we had come to Jerusalem, the brethren received
us gladly. ¹⁸On the following day Paul went in with us to
James; and all the elders were present. ¹⁹After greeting them,
he related one by one the things that God had done among the
Gentiles through his ministry. ²⁰And when they heard it, they
glorified God. And they said to him, "You see, brother, how
many thousands there are among the Jews of those who have
believed; they are all zealous for the law, ²¹and they have been
told about you that you teach all the Jews who are among the
Gentiles to forsake Moses, telling them not to circumcise their
children or observe the customs.

Arrival in Jerusalem, 21:15, 16

[15, 16] From **Caesarea** they **went up to Jerusalem**.
Certain disciples from there led Paul and his fellow workers
to the house of Mnason of Cyprus. Mnason was probably
notable in Luke's story because he was an early disciple.
The group chose to **lodge** with him (Acts 9:11; 16:15; 21:8).

Meeting with James, 21:17-21

[17-20a] Luke depicts an irenic situation existing between Paul and his party and the leaders at Jerusalem.
James and all the elders **gladly received** them. After the
greeting Paul related what had been accomplished by **God
among the Gentiles**. Paul reported at Jerusalem following all
three of his missionary journeys (15:2; 18:22; 21:15) even
though Antioch was his true base of operations. He did this
so that good communications related to the contested
aspects of the Gentile mission might be secured and maintained and also so that **God** might be **glorified** (11:18).

[20b, 21] Jerusalem's consent and support of the Gentile
mission did not preclude problems. The leaders of Jewish

²²**What then is to be done? They will certainly hear that you have come.**

Christianity at Jerusalem reported to Paul, though he surely needed no reminder, that there were **many thousands** of **Jews who believed**. And since they all, including Pharisaic believers (15:5), were **zealous for the law**, understandable confusion, discord, and hostility could occur.

The rumor was circulated among these Jewish Christians that Paul was teaching **all the Jews who are among the Gentiles** (i.e., diaspora) **to forsake Moses**. This included telling **them not to circumcise their children or observe the customs** (*ēthos* = sacred ordinances in Luke 1:9; 2:42; John 19:40; Acts 6:14; 15:1; 21:21; 26:3; 28:17). Of course this report was totally false as is proven not only by Paul's efforts here to quash it (21:23-26) but even more powerfully by his own writings. Paul never forbade or taught against the circumcision of a Jew (or in Timothy's case, a half-Jew, Acts 16:1-3), if it was done for the reasons set forth in scripture. Since the Jewish scriptures never taught that circumcision and sacred **customs** were the basis of acquiring God's righteousness, Paul opposed all theories and forms of works-righteousness based on keeping these.

The apostle's attitude toward Gentile believers and the Jewish laws was a different matter. The only imaginable reason for a Gentile believer of Paul's day to endure circumcision would have been that he believed it was necessary for salvation or at least a touchstone of one's piety. This religious system of human precepts and doctrines, of a philosophy of sensuous minds and beguiling reason, and of sectarianism was effectively overturned by Paul in his letters to the churches of Galatia and Colossae.

James' Advice, 21:22-25

[22] James and the elders were worried, for there was no way to hide Paul's presence from the believing Jews. **They** would **hear that** he had come.

²³**Do therefore what we tell you. We have four men who are under a vow; ²⁴take these men and purify yourself along with them and pay their expenses, so that they may shave their heads.**

---

[23] The pragmatic solution arrived at was that Paul should participate in a Jewish custom, **a vow**, thereby demonstrating the falseness of the charges (21:21) and silencing the opposition. Apparently they picked, without long deliberation, **four men** (this vow was open to women, Num. 6:2) who were **under a vow**.

[24a] Paul was enjoined to do two things: to **purify** himself **along with them** and to **pay their expenses**. To **purify** (*hagnizō*) oneself in a Nazirite **vow** (see comments on Acts 18:18 and below) meant different things at different times in the duration of the **vow**, ranging from abstinence from haircuts, grape juice, raisins, vinegar, and wine at the beginning, to a haircut, to animal sacrifice at the end (Num. 6:1-21). The "seven days" mentioned in Acts 21:27 probably referred to the purification required of accidental defilement occurring during the **vow** (Num. 6:9, "on the seventh day he shall shave it"). This would mean that the **expenses** Paul was required to **pay** were for "two turtledoves or two young pigeons" which were sacrificed to purify the unintentionally incurred defilement (Num. 6:10-12). Clearly, then, Paul helped Jewish Christians participate in the sacrificial system set forth by Moses. Prominent Jewish leaders from time to time defrayed the expenses of large numbers of Nazirites as an act of charity (Josephus, *Antiquities* XIX. 294).

The obvious problem raised by this episode has been handled in various ways. J. W. McGarvey (*Commentary on Acts*, vol. 2, pp. 208, 209) asserted that Paul could not have done this consistently and with integrity had he already known the truths of the subsequently written epistles to the Ephesians and the Hebrews (sic). The points about the abolishing of the priestly sacrificial system,

Thus all will know that there is nothing in what they have been told about you but that you yourself live in observance of the law. ²⁵ **But as for the Gentiles who have believed, we have sent a letter with our judgment that they should abstain from what has been sacrificed to idols and from blood and from what is strangled**^y **and from unchastity."**

^yOther early authorities omit *and from what is strangled*

McGarvey admits, "had not yet been clearly revealed to his mind, and much less to the minds of the other disciples." In this way Paul was not unlike Peter, who was guided by the Holy Spirit into all the truth, not in a single bound, but step by step. Just as Peter needed the Cornelius incident to reveal to him the full implication of what he already knew (Acts 1:8; 2:39), so the older Paul (of Ephesians and Hebrews) realized some truth he had not known at this juncture of his life. Another possibility is that Paul's irenic and accommodating practice (cf. 1 Cor. 9:20-22) of flexibility was responsible for this action. Given this solution it would follow that, like circumcision, the practice of the Jewish sacrificial system (which became a dead issue after A.D. 70) was reckoned apostasy only when it was regarded as necessary for salvation or undermined the work of Christ on the cross (Col. 1:20; Rom. 3:25; 1 Cor. 5:7).

[24b] Paul's action was designated by Luke a demonstration of the fact that he lived **in observance of the law**.

[25] As though to emphasize the fact that all of this has to do only with Jewish Christians the statement is made, almost parenthetically, **But as for the Gentiles . . . .** The regulations **for Gentiles** was an issue already treated in a **letter** in Acts 15. It was the same letter of judgment mentioned here.

V

Paul's Years of Imprisonment
21:26–28:31

PAUL ARRESTED IN JERUSALEM, 21:26–23:22

Paul in the Temple, 21:26-31

[26] Once again Luke mentions the particulars of how the vow was regulated and Paul's part in it. Paul was **purified** (*hagnizō*), entered **the temple**, and gave **notice** to the sacerdotal officials. The **offering** (*prosphora*) specifically mentioned here referred to the male and ewe lamb, one ram, and drink and meal (cereal) offering (Num. 6:14, 15).

[27] Before this vow could be completed, **when the seven days were almost completed**, pandemonium broke out. It was not, however, from the source James had anticipated. It was not Jewish believers but rather **Jews from Asia**. Diaspora **Jews**, Hellenists who had opposed and hounded Paul from the beginning (cf. Acts 9:29), had found him once again. Paul, **in the temple** in an attempt to reduce Jewish Christian suspicions, was seen there by unbelieving Jews. They incited **the crowd** and **laid hands on** Paul.

125

²⁶Then Paul took the men, and the next day he purified himself with them and went into the temple, to give notice when the days of purification would be fulfilled and the offering presented for every one of them.

²⁷When the seven days were almost completed, the Jews from Asia, who had seen him in the temple, stirred up all the crowd, and laid hands on him, ²⁸crying out, "Men of Israel, help! This is the man who is teaching men everywhere against the people and the law and this place; moreover he also brought Greeks into the temple, and he has defiled this holy place." ²⁹For they had previously seen Trophimus the Ephesian with him in the city, and they supposed that Paul had brought him into the temple. ³⁰Then all the city was aroused, and the people ran together; they seized Paul and dragged him out of the temple, and at once the gates were shut.

---

[28] Crying, "help!" the Jews charged Paul with **teaching men everywhere against the people** (i.e., Israel), **against the law**, and **against this place** (i.e., the temple). These were the stock Jewish charges against Jesus and the early Christians (cf. Mark 14:56-64; John 2:19; Acts 6:13, 14; etc.).

Another unfounded accusation was that Paul brought Gentiles **into the temple**, thereby having **defiled this holy place**. This was a grievous offense in Judaism, which carried a commensurate penalty (see note on 21:31).

[29] Luke briefly explained how such a mistaken claim could have been made. A certain Gentile Christian in Paul's entourage named **Trophimus** (called an Asian in Acts 20:4; cf. 2 Tim. 4:20) had, **they supposed, been brought** by the apostle **into the temple**.

[30] Chaos and rage spread through **the city** and the **people ran together** (cf. 19:29). To Paul's total bewilderment he was **dragged out of the temple**. No word is provided on the whereabouts of Trophimus or the four men under a vow. The **gates** of the temple **were shut**, probably by the captain of the temple (Acts 4:1) to preclude further violence.

[31]And as they were trying to kill him, word came to the tribune of the cohort that all Jerusalem was in confusion. [32]He at once took soldiers and centurions, and ran down to them; and when they saw the tribune and the soldiers, they stopped beating Paul.

---

[31] The livid mob was **trying to kill** Paul. There was no problem with Gentiles entering the outer court of the temple precinct. There was an inner second court, however, beyond which Gentiles could not proceed. Along the wall of demarcation between these two courts there were bilingual warnings that it was a capital offense for Gentiles to pass beyond that point (Josephus, *War* V.v.2; cf. *Antiquities* XV.xi.5; even a Roman citizen could be killed for such a violation, *War* VI.ii.4). Some of the ancient stone slabs which contained these warnings have been discovered in modern times. They were explicit that whoever was caught in violation of these prohibitions would be liable to the mandatory death penalty.

Luke next introduces the reader **to the tribune of the cohort**, later identified as Claudius Lysias (23:26). The **word** that came to him probably originated with the guards who regularly kept watch over the temple precinct (Josephus, *War* V.v.8). During pilgrimage festivals when the city was crowded, these guards were especially alert to altercations and disruptions. Since the Roman soldiers were garrisoned in the fortress of Antonia (see Josephus, *War* V.v.8) adjacent to the sanctuary, they could quickly respond to problems. The Antonia was an old Jewish fortress rebuilt by Herod the Great (Josephus, *Antiquities* XIII.xi.2) and named for Mark Antony.

Paul Rescued by Romans, 21:32-36

[32] Realizing the volatile nature of Jewish riots in the temple area during festival periods, **the tribune** responded in force. **He took soldiers**, and, if the literalness of **centurions** is pressed, he was accompanied by at least two hundred men.

³³**Then the tribune came up and arrested him, and ordered him to be bound with two chains. He inquired who he was and what he had done.** ³⁴**Some in the crowd shouted one thing, some another; and as he could not learn the facts because of the uproar, he ordered him to be brought into the barracks.** ³⁵**And when he came to the steps, he was actually carried by the soldiers because of the violence of the crowd;** ³⁶**for the mob of the people followed, crying, "Away with him!"**

³⁷**As Paul was about to be brought into the barracks, he said to the tribune, "May I say something to you?" And he said, "Do you know Greek?**

The expression **ran down** indicates that they descended from the Antonia by one of the two stairways which connected the fortress to the temple (cf. 21:35, 40; Josephus, *War* V.v.8). When the **soldiers** arrived, the Jews **stopped beating Paul**.

[33] The **tribune arrested** Paul, confident, it seems, that he was indeed guilty of some heinous crime. It served, however, to take Paul into protective custody. Paul was **bound with two chains** and handcuffed to a soldier on each arm (cf. Acts 12:6). Next Claudius Lysias inquired **who** Paul **was** and **what he had done.**

[34] The tumultuous **crowd** was unable to present a clear case of the facts. The **crowd** itself was divided and confused (as at Ephesus, Acts 19:32). Since the tribune could not even **learn the facts**, he had Paul **brought into the barracks** (i.e., Antonia).

[35, 36] To intensify the fact that pandemonium reigned Luke adds that Paul **actually** had to be **carried** above **the mob** by the Roman **soldiers**. There was pitched violence and the crowd followed after them **crying** for Paul's death, **"Away with him!"** (cf. Acts 22:22; Luke 23:18; John 19:15; *Martyrdom of Polycarp* 3:1; 9:2).

Paul the Citizen, 21:37-40

[37] Before the apostle was brought **into the barracks,**

128

³⁸**Are you not the Egyptian, then, who recently stirred up a revolt and led the four thousand men of the Assassins out into the wilderness?"** ³⁹**Paul replied, "I am a Jew, from Tarsus in Cilicia, a citizen of no mean city; I beg you, let me speak to the people."**

---

he asked the **tribune, "May I say something to you?"** The tribune was surprised that Paul knew **Greek.**

[38] Paul was immediately asked, **"Are you not the Egyptian, then?"** The tribune's query was evoked by the tumult and Paul's ability to speak Greek, thereby suggesting he was foreign. The **Egyptian** to whom Claudius Lysias referred had recently started a **revolt** and led a band of **Assassins into the wilderness.** This type of insurrection was not infrequent in Judea in the third quarter of the first century. The word **Assassins** was rendered from the Greek term *sikarios*, whose etymological meaning (from Latin *sica*) was "dagger man" or assassin. This band of terrorists assassinated their enemies in broad daylight. Concealing their assassin's blade under their clothes, they could therefore murder people in crowds without detection. Scores were killed (including Jonathan the high priest), in the temple as well as on the city streets (Josephus, *War* II.xiii.3-4; *Antiquities* XX.viii.5).

Josephus recorded an episode of an **Egyptian** false prophet whose insurrection closely paralleled that of the Egyptian mentioned by Claudius Lysias. This Egyptian (*Antiquities* XX.viii.6; *War* II.xiii.5) was a self-proclaimed prophet who thought he could perform wonders and thereby rout the Roman occupational forces. He led a group of followers to the mount of Olives. Felix heard about this intended coup and sent Roman infantry to abort the revolt. Most of the Egyptian's forces were killed or captured, but he himself escaped, though certainly with a reward on his head.

[39] Paul quickly replied that he was a **Jew** (cf. Phil. 3:5, 6; 2 Cor. 11:22) and a **citizen** of **Tarsus in**

⁴⁰And when he had given him leave, Paul, standing on the steps, motioned with his hand to the people; and when there was a great hush, he spoke to them in the Hebrew language, saying:

¹"Brethren and fathers, hear the defense which I now make before you."

Cilicia. The apostle also expressed (in Greek idiom indicative of some pride) that **Tarsus** was **no mean city. Tarsus** was a city of pre-eminence, both culturally and politically. It was visited by several Roman emperors during the imperial period and was the burial site of Julian the Apostate. The ancient geographer Strabo observed that **Tarsus** had surpassed both Athens and Alexandria in the fields of philosophy, rhetoric, and general education (*Geography* 14.5.13).

Paul mentioned at this point only his citizenship of Tarsus, waiting until later (cf. Acts 16:37) to inform Claudius Lysias of his Roman citizenship (22:25). Dual citizenship (if Roman citizenship was involved) was expressly forbidden by Roman law of an earlier period (Cicero, *In Defense of Lucius Corneilius Balbus* 28-29). Under the early empire, however, dual citizenship was permissible.

Paul begged to **speak to** the raging mob. Since his best effort to placate the misinformed Jewish Christians and to obviate general Jewish hostility had failed, he decided to make a defense of his actions and practices (22:1).

[40] Given leave to speak, **Paul** quieted the crowd with **his hand** (cf. 13:16; 19:33) and **spoke to them in the Hebrew language**, more precisely in Aramaic, the common tongue of Judea.

Paul's Address to Jews in Jerusalem, 22:1-21

Paul's Upbringing, 22:1-5. [1] Brethren and fathers is typical style for Jewish audiences (cf. Acts 2:29; 7:2; 13:26; 15:7, 13; 23:1, 6; 28:17).

² And when they heard that he addressed them in the Hebrew language, they were the more quiet. And he said:

³ "I am a Jew, born at Tarsus in Cilicia, but brought up in this city at the feet of Gamaliel, educated according to the strict manner of the law of our fathers, being zealous for God as you all are this day.

Defense (*apologia*) was a key term in both this speech and the remainder of Acts. More than one commentator has pointed out that from a certain perspective the latter chapters of Acts are a legal **defense** for Paul. This must surely have been central to Luke's overall apologetic interests (see part 1, pp. 15–17). It is also noteworthy that in reference to Paul the verb and noun forms for the term **defense** begin in 22:1 and are sprinkled throughout the remainder of Acts (e.g., 24:10; 25:8, 16; 26:1, 2, 24). Furthermore, it is indicative of Luke's interest that he filled as many chapters with the legal processes, maneuvers, and trials of Paul as he had used for all of Paul's missionary journeys.

[2] **Hebrew language** (Aramaic) was used by Paul to gain better attention and respect from his audience, since it was their own tongue.

[3a] This section begins the second of three Pauline conversion accounts in Acts, each one narrated for a different audience (see notes on Acts 9:1ff., as parallel material will not be treated again).

Even though born at **Tarsus**, Paul was reared and educated abroad (as so many from Tarsus were) in Jerusalem. **Gamaliel** (grandson of the famous Rabbi Hillel) was an influential member of the Jewish council and apparently more tolerant in matters of religious pluralism (Acts 5:33-39) than his pupil Saul.

[3b] As will be demonstrated below, Paul was especially concerned in this account of his conversion to set forth the Jewishness of his life, conversion, and commission by God. The ensuing events make it clear why the apostle would choose such a strategic and expedient perspective.

131

⁴**I persecuted this Way to the death, binding and delivering to prison both men and women, ⁵ as the high priest and the whole council of elders bear me witness. From them I received letters to the brethren, and I journeyed to Damascus to take those also who were there and bring them in bonds to Jerusalem to be punished.**

He first related that his religious training was orthodox **according to the manner of the law of our fathers** (cf. 24:14). In a religion and culture so structured around the patriarch, reference to the **fathers** was important (cf. Matt. 3:9; 23:30; Acts 3:13, 25; 4:25; 5:30; 7:11; 13:17, 32; 15:10; 22:14; 26:6; 28:25). The word used is *patrōos*, meaning ancestral or inherited from one's father (Acts 22:3; 24:14; 28:17; *3 Maccabees* 1:23; *4 Maccabees* 16:16).

Paul was also **zealous for God** (cf. especially Gal. 1:14; Phil. 3:6), as were the hostile Jews to whom he spoke. Just as Paul had earlier complimented the Athenians on the religiosity manifested by their idolatry (Acts 17:22), here he noted the zeal **for God** which the unbelieving Jews had. Not many months prior to this episode Paul had written concerning the unbelieving Jews: "I bear them witness that they have a zeal for God" (Rom. 10:2; cf. Acts 21:20 for believing Jews' zeal for the law).

[4] Saul's persecution of the church is narrated in Acts 8:1-3 and 9:1ff. (see notes there) and recounted by Paul himself (cf. 22:20; 26:10; 1 Cor. 15:9; Gal. 1:13; Phil. 3:6; 1 Tim. 1:13). **Way** was a frequent name for Christians (see notes on Acts 9:2).

[5] Present knowledge of Jewish legal practices and prerogatives in the Empire is lamentably cloudy and sparse. Apparently the **high priest** and **whole council of elders** (Sanhedrin; also Luke 22:66; cf. Acts 4:5, 15) had power to imprison, but it is debated whether they had the power of capital punishment (cf. John 18:31). It is unclear on what grounds the Christians would have been brought **in bonds to Jerusalem to be punished**. The multiplicity of sects tolerated

⁶"As I made my journey and drew near to Damascus, about noon a great light from heaven suddenly shone about me. ⁷And I fell to the ground and heard a voice saying to me, 'Saul, Saul, why do you persecute me?' ⁸And I answered, 'Who are you, Lord?' And he said to me, 'I am Jesus of Nazareth whom you are persecuting.' ⁹Now those who were with me saw the light but did not hear the voice of the one who was speaking to me.

---

within first century Judaism and the lack of regimentation in Jewish beliefs make one wonder, from a strictly legal perspective, why these Jews were harassed and imprisoned and the Jews of the Dead Sea community (the Essenes), for example, were not. Both groups denounced the other manifestations of Judaism as evil and polluted and proclaimed themselves the true remnant and heir of the Old Testament. Perhaps the reason behind the extraordinary hostility by the Jewish hierarchy toward Jewish believers in Christ was that unlike the eschatalogical community at Qumran, the Jewish Christians remained in the world. The former chose to give their corporate witness in the desert wilderness; the latter, in Jerusalem, Judea, Samaria, and to the end of the earth. One walked the highways and byways of the world; the other dwelt principally near the unpopulated shores of the Dead Sea.

Paul's Conversion, 22:6-16. [6, 7] The appearance of the Lord occurred **about noon** (midday, 26:13) and was accompanied by a blinding light **from heaven** (cf. Acts 12:7). The Bible often connects the imagery of light with God's presence (e.g., 1 Tim. 6:16; Rev. 21:22-24; 22:5). This momentous encounter between the recalcitrant **Saul** and the Lord Jesus brings to one's mind that great verse "The people who walked in darkness have seen a great light; those who dwelt in a land of deep darkness, on them has light shined" (Isa. 9:2).

[8, 9] Paul, uncertain of the origin of the **voice** and **light**, cried out, **"Who are you?"** **"Jesus of Nazareth"** was the

¹⁰And I said, 'What shall I do, Lord?' And the Lord said to me, 'Rise, and go into Damascus, and there you will be told all that is appointed for you to do.' ¹¹And when I could not see because of the brightness of that light, I was led by the hand by those who were with me, and came into Damascus.
¹²"And one Ananias, a devout man according to the law, well spoken of by all the Jews who lived there,

---

reply. This brief exchange centered upon the term **persecuting**. Paul obviously had not persecuted Jesus of Nazareth during the "days of his flesh." Nevertheless, to persecute the followers of Christ was to persecute Christ. To reject a messenger of God was to reject God himself (Ex. 4:16; 1 Sam. 8:7; Matt. 10:40; Luke 10:16; John 12:44; 13:20). While it is interesting to speculate that this identification of the **persecuting** of Christians and Jesus reflected the fuller Pauline concept of the body of Christ (e.g., Col. 1:18), it cannot be cogently demonstrated. Jesus' statement only need reflect the above mentioned concept that he who rejects the servant of a master also rejects the master.

For the actions of those who accompanied Saul, see notes on Acts 9:7.

[10, 11] Paul asked, **"Lord what shall I do?"** (cf. 9:6). It yet remained for Paul **to do** what was **appointed**. He must continue to Damascus to learn the will of God for him. No doubt Paul was fully convicted on the road to Damascus, but he was converted in the city of Damascus.

The **brightness of** the **light** temporarily blinded Paul. How different was his entry into **Damascus** from what he had expected. No longer the confident defender of the faith, zealous for traditions; rather, blind and confused he must be **led by the hand**, like a child, into Damascus.

[12] In the description of **Ananias**, Luke, like Paul, stresses those facts which would have appeal mostly to a Jewish audience. Thus in this account one learns that **Ananias** was **devout according to the law**, whereas in other

¹³came to me, and standing by me said to me, 'Brother Saul,
receive your sight.' And in that very hour I received my sight
and saw him. ¹⁴And he said, 'The God of our fathers
appointed you to know his will, to see the Just One and to hear
a voice from his mouth; ¹⁵for you will be a witness for him to
all men of what you have seen and heard. ¹⁶And now why do
you wait? Rise and be baptized, and wash away your sins,
calling on his name.'

---

situations the narrative calls him merely a disciple
(= Christian, Acts 9:6) or omits the reference to him
(26:16ff.). Moreover, Paul related here that this law-keeping
believer was **well spoken of by all the Jews** in Damascus.

[13] Ananias **came to** Paul and miraculously restored his
sight (cf. 9:17, 18). The apostle's **sight** was regained within
the **hour** (cf. 9:18, immediately).

[14, 15] These verses contain a unique account of Paul's
apostolic commissioning (see also Rom. 11:13; 15:15-21;
1 Cor. 15:8-10; Gal. 1:15, 16; Eph. 3:8-10). The Jewish
motif **God of our fathers** was employed as well as the
descriptive title **Just One** (cf. Acts 3:14; 7:52; James 5:6;
1 John 2:1; canonical and noncanonical Jewish literature of
antiquity stressed the righteous quality of God's servant;
cf. also the attitudes of Pilate's wife in Matt. 27:19 and the
centurion in Luke 23:47).

To know his will expressed a common desire in Jewish
piety (Rom. 2:18; 12:2; Col. 1:9) and would lead one to do
God's **will** (Pss. 40:8; 143:10). **Witness** to the risen Lord was,
of course, at the core of Luke's composition of Acts (see
1:8).

[16] As all other Christians in the apostolic era, Paul **was
baptized** to **wash away** his **sins** (Acts 2:38; 9:18; 1 Cor. 6:11;
Eph. 5:26; Titus 3:5). Immersion was accompanied by an
invoking or **calling on his name** (Matt. 28:19; Acts 2:21; 9:14;
Rom. 10:13; cf. Eph. 5:26 and the expression "with the
word").

¹⁷ "When I had returned to Jerusalem and was praying in the temple, I fell into a trance ¹⁸ and saw him saying to me, 'Make haste and get quickly out of Jerusalem, because they will not accept your testimony about me.' ¹⁹ And I said, 'Lord, they themselves know that in every synagogue I imprisoned and beat those who believed in thee. ²⁰ And when the blood of Stephen thy witness was shed, I also was standing by and approving, and keeping the garments of those who killed him.'

Paul's Commission to Go to Gentiles, 22:17-21. [17] The reader is totally surprised when Luke next reports that Paul **returned to Jerusalem**. Obviously Paul had no interest in further alienating his audience in the temple area by recapitulating his bout with the synagogue at Damascus (Acts 9:19b-25). Furthermore, Paul still strove to demonstrate when called upon that his commission, that is, the Gentile mission, was rooted in scripture (see notes on 13:46, 47) and supported by the **Jerusalem** leadership of the church. Accordingly Paul mentioned at this juncture (and only here) that his Gentile ministry was revealed to him in no other place than the **Jerusalem temple** itself. And it came not from the twelve (cf. Gal. 1:1ff.), nor was it a stratagem to get Paul out of Palestine (a thing reckoned desirable by some, Acts 9:26-31). Rather his knowledge of God's will for him to preach to the Gentiles came during a moment of ecstasy and revelation (cf. 2 Cor. 12:1-7) when he **fell into a trance** (*ekstasis*, cf. Acts 3:10; 10:10; 11:5; 22:17) **in the temple**.

[18-20] Paul at this point left his conciliatory tenor and emphatically asserted the persistence of Jewish disbelief. God had urged Paul to **get quickly out of Jerusalem**. God, the heart knower, knew well that the Jews would not accept Paul's testimony about him.

The apostle still possessed a naive optimism and incredulity about Jewish disbelief. He argued with God that since his conversion had been so radical the Jews would have to listen because of his sincerity and devotion. Previously Paul

²¹ And he said to me, 'Depart; for I will send you far away to the Gentiles.' "

²² Up to this word they listened to him; then they lifted up their voices and said, "Away with such a fellow from the earth! For he ought not to live." ²³ And as they cried out and waved their garments and threw dust into the air, ²⁴ the tribune commanded him to be brought into the barracks, and ordered him to be examined by scourging, to find out why they shouted thus against him.

---

had **imprisoned** and **beat** believers. He had even approved those who **shed the blood of Stephen** (cf. 7:58). The truth of the gospel, however, did not rest, as Paul himself knew (Gal. 1:8), upon one's sincerity, radical devotion, or drastic quality of conversion. What Paul's about-face did demonstrate (beyond scaring some Jewish Christians, 9:26) was that God's love can justify the ungodly (Rom. 4:5), and save disobedient people in virtue of his mercy (1 Tim. 1:13, 14).

[21] God's wisdom was wiser than Paul's ambition and hopes for his brethren of the flesh (cf. Rom. 9:1-3). He commanded Paul to **depart**. The temple revelation ended with God's injunction **I will send you far away to the Gentiles**. Volatile though it would be, Paul concluded this sermon with a mandate for the Gentile mission. Christian expediency had its limits, and the apostle refused to deny this divine directive even when facing a bloodthirsty crowd bent on his death.

Turmoil in Jerusalem, 22:22-29

[22] The Jewish audience heard the **word** about Gentiles. At that point they became greatly indignant, crying out for the apostle's life (cf. 21:36).

[23] **They cried out, waved their garments** (cf. 14:14; 18:6), and **threw dust into the air** to reflect their disgust and horror at the apostle's word.

[24] The **tribune** was still confused about Paul and the Jews' reaction to him, all the more so since he probably

²⁵**But when they had tied him up with the thongs, Paul said to the centurion who was standing by, "Is it lawful for you to scourge a man who is a Roman citizen, and uncondemned?"** ²⁶**When the centurion heard that, he went to the tribune and said to him, "What are you about to do? For this man is a Roman citizen."**

---

could not understand Paul's Aramaic sermon. Having Paul **examined by scourging** reflected a frequently used Roman method of interrogation of slaves and lower classes of freedmen. Roman **scourging** here was not for punishment, but rather a truth serum of sorts. Two ancient documents of Roman law, *Lex Porcia* and *Lex Iulia*, prohibited the torture, scourge, condemnation or killing of an uncondemned Roman citizen (cf. Acts 16:37; 25:16), but the law was on occasion breached (see Paulus, *Sententiae* 5.26.1; Ulpian, *Digest* 48.6.7; Livy, *History of Rome* 10.9.4).

[25] When **they tied** Paul up to scourge him, he spoke out to a nearby **centurion** concerning the legality of scourging an **uncondemned Roman citizen.** As noted above, this was illegal. One vivid account from the writings of Cicero is pertinent here. Cicero reported that a certain Roman citizen named Gavius was abused by the corrupt Roman governor of Sicily, a man named Verres. During the agony of public beating with rods all that came from Gavius' lips were the words "I am a Roman citizen," by which he hoped to shield himself from the blows. The privileges and glory of Roman citizenship were known throughout the Mediterranean basin. Continuing his emotional attack upon Verres, Cicero remarked, "It is an outrage to bind a Roman citizen, detestable to scourge him, an infamous murder to kill him—what shall I say—to crucify a Roman citizen?" (*Against Verres* 2.5.161–170).

[26] With this example in mind (cf. 22:29) one can appreciate the response of the **centurion** to Paul's protest. The **centurion** went to the **tribune** with the serious question, **What are you about to do?**

²⁷So the tribune came and said to him, "Tell me, are you a Roman citizen?" And he said, "Yes." ²⁸The tribune answered, "I bought this citizenship for a large sum." Paul said, "But I was born a citizen." ²⁹So those who were about to examine him withdrew from him instantly; and the tribune also was afraid, for he realized that Paul was a Roman citizen and that he had bound him.

---

[27] The **tribune** was also aware of the legal and political implications of this act. He immediately asked Paul, **"Are you a Roman citizen?"**

[28] To further question Paul the **tribune** commented that he also was a Roman citizen, his **citizenship** having been purchased. Later Dio Cassius (60.17.5ff.) related, though in exaggerated style, that the practice of purchasing Roman **citizenship** had been initiated under the early empire. Claudius Lysias questioned the apostle to insure that Paul was not lying. Some made false claims to Roman citizenship in antiquity and frequently paid for it with their life, if discovered (see Suetonius, *Life of Claudius* 25.3; Epictetus, *Discourses* III.24.41).

Paul retorted that he **was born a** Roman **citizen**. We do not know under what circumstances Paul's ancestors acquired this status.

[29] **Those about to examine** Paul by scourging immediately **withdrew**. Notable is a parallel in the famous *Letters* of Pliny-Trajan, which record the treatment of Christians by the Roman officials in the area of Pontus and Bithynia (*Letters* 10.96, 97). There the delegate Pliny wrote to the Emperor Trajan to inform him concerning his own treatment of Christians. In the course of the report Pliny mentioned that "he believed it was all the more necessary to interrogate by means of torture two slave women, called deaconesses" (10.96.8) in order to obtain correct information about the nature of the Christian religion.

The value of the tribune's citizenship was vulnerable if he violated Paul's. This scene fitted nicely into Luke's

³⁰**But on the morrow, desiring to know the real reason why the Jews accused him, he unbound him, and commanded the chief priests and all the council to meet, and he brought Paul down and set him before them.**

¹**And Paul, looking intently at the council, said, "Brethren, I have lived before God in all good conscience up to this day."** ²**And the high priest Ananias commanded those who stood by him to strike him on the mouth.** ³**Then Paul said to him, "God shall strike you, you whitewashed wall! Are you sitting to judge me according to the law, and yet contrary to the law you order me to be struck?"**

---

apologetic concern about the legal status of the church in the Empire. Furthermore, Luke's statement **that he had bound him** was powerful to a Roman audience familiar with the sentiment of Cicero cited at verse 25.

Paul before the Sanhedrin, 22:30–23:10

[30] These next eleven verses depict Paul's defense and witness before the Jewish Sanhedrin. With Paul in custody the tribune was in an awkward position legally, as indeed were all Roman officials who arrested or tried Christians (see especially Pliny-Trajan, *Letters* 10.96.1ff.). He wanted to ascertain **the real reason** (cf. 18:14-16) **why the Jews** attempted to kill Paul. A Roman could not be detained indefinitely, much less sentenced (cf. 25:16), without knowing the charges on which he was accused.

[1] **Paul** immediately declared that a good conscience (*suneidēsis agathē*) had characterized all of his activities up to that point (cf. 2 Tim. 1:3). Although **conscience** is not the final judge of right and wrong (1 Cor. 4:4), Paul knew well that it was the only human faculty for evaluating guidance and direction (see Acts 24:16; Rom. 13:5; 1 Cor. 8:7, 10, 12; 10:25-29; 2 Cor. 1:12; 4:2; 1 Tim. 1:5, 19; 3:9; 4:2; 2 Tim. 1:3; Titus 1:15).

[2, 3] The treatment of Paul here is reminiscent of the travesty Jesus endured before Pilate and the Jews. By

⁴**Those who stood by said, "Would you revile God's high priest?" ⁵And Paul said, "I did not know, brethren, that he was the high priest; for it is written, 'You shall not speak evil of a ruler of your people.' "**

modern Western standards many trials in antiquity would be considered kangaroo court, and the trials of Christians were no exception.

Ananias, appointed **high priest** by Herod in A.D. 47, had Paul struck **on the mouth** (cf. John 18:22). The outraged apostle retorted to **Ananias, "God shall strike you."** This curse came to fruition when Ananias was assassinated in A.D. 66 by zealous anti-Roman Jews in Jerusalem. The background imagery for Paul's retort was not Jesus' words about **whitewashed** tombs (Matt. 23:27). Rather, the prophetic utterances in Ezekiel 13:10-16 provide the appropriate symbolism of a **wall whitewashed** by false leaders of Israel. **God** told Ezekiel that he himself would **strike** and destroy this **whitewashed wall** as well as those who daubed it with whitewash. Paul's statement is replete, then, with insinuations about the falseness of **Ananias** and his colleagues and their fate at the hand of **God**.

Paul specifically noted the travesty of justice manifested in the high priest's attempt to **judge according to the law, yet** being **contrary to the law.** The precept of Leviticus 19:15, "You shall do no injustice in judgment," lies behind Paul's charge.

[4, 5] Next the apostle was accused of reviling **God's high priest**, a clear violation of Exodus 22:28, "You shall not revile God, nor curse a ruler of your people." Several suggestions have been offered regarding the meaning and logic of Paul's response, **I did not know.** One theory is that Paul was sincerely apologizing, thereby showing his obedience to the law. Others have opined that he was looking in another direction and had not known who uttered the words against him. A further suggestion is that Paul, having been away from Jerusalem since Ananias had become **high priest**,

⁶**But when Paul perceived that one part were Sadducees and the other Pharisees, he cried out in the council, "Brethren, I am a Pharisee, a son of Pharisees; with respect to the hope and the resurrection of the dead I am on trial." ⁷And when he had said this, a dissension arose between the Pharisees and the Sadducees; and the assembly was divided. ⁸For the Sadducees say that there is no resurrection, nor angel, nor spirit; but the Pharisees acknowledge them all.**

---

did not recognize who he was. Another theory is that Paul's bad eyesight (cf. Gal. 4:15; 6:11) kept him from recognizing Ananias.

These interpretations seem at best tendentious and rob the text of its clearest meaning. Here is an example of the apostle's vitriolic sarcasm. This bellicose exchange was cut from the same cloth as Paul's suggestion of castration to Judaizers (Gal. 5:12) and his biting sarcasm reflected in 2 Corinthians 10–13. Anger had its place in Paul's doctrine (Eph. 4:26) and the apostle, like his Lord (cf. Matt. 23:13-33; Mark 3:5), knew that it was no transgression to speak the truth. The rhetorical logic of Paul's answer (notice the **for** [*gar*] in 23:5b) is that since it was unlawful to **revile God's high priest** and Paul had just reviled Ananias, Ananias must not be God's faithful **high priest**.

[6] With great agility the defendant Paul took the offensive. Trained as a Pharisee (Phil. 3:5; Gal. 1:14) Paul was well aware of the distinctive beliefs of the **Pharisees** and the **Sadducees**. He declared that the issue before the council was really **the hope** of **the resurrection**. One could hardly fault the apostle for bringing forward this doctrine since his assessment of the issue was far more accurate than that of his detractors. Of course the doctrine of the **resurrection** was not the specific doctrine that brought Paul to this **trial** (21:28-30; 22:22), but it was a true source of irritation among the Sadducees (Acts 4:2).

[7, 8] With Paul's claim a predictable **dissension arose between the Pharisees and the Sadducees**. The apostle knew

⁹Then a great clamor arose; and some of the scribes of the Pharisees' party stood up and contended, "We find nothing wrong in this man. What if a spirit or an angel spoke to him?" ¹⁰And when the dissension became violent, the tribune, afraid that Paul would be torn in pieces by them, commanded the soldiers to go down and take him by force from among them and bring him into the barracks.

¹¹The following night the Lord stood by him and said, "Take courage, for as you have testified about me at Jerusalem, so you must be a witness also at Rome."

---

the philosophy of divide and conquer. Luke informs his readers that the **Sadducees**, unlike the **Pharisees**, believed there was **no resurrection, nor angel, nor spirit**. These were not the only issues over which they were **divided** (cf. Josephus, *War* II.viii.14; *Antiquities* XVIII.i.2; Matt. 22:23; Mark 12:18; Luke 20:27), but they were three pertinent to the ensuing argument.

[9] His remarks provided such a catalyst that **a great clamor arose**. Both Jewish parties had **scribes** or scholars of scripture (cf. Mark 2:16; Luke 5:30; 20:19). The **Pharisees** exonerated their fellow Pharisee, Paul. Perhaps, they reasoned, **a spirit** or **angel** had spoken to Paul on the road to Damascus. To deny this possibility was tantamount to conceding that the Sadducees were right, a concession not quickly made by the **Pharisees**.

[10] We do not know whether Paul hoped that the clamor would become so **violent**. The **tribune** once again rescued Paul (21:31, 32; 22:22). The **soldiers** had to take him by force **from among** the savage council and return him to **the barracks** (cf. 21:34; 22:24).

A Plot Against Paul's Life, 23:11-22

[11] God **stood by** Paul at this hour of crisis as he had done before in Corinth (18:9). **Take courage** (*tharseō*; cf. Matt. 14:27; John 16:33) was the revelation. The apostle's ministry was not at its end. Just as he had **testified**

¹²When it was day, the Jews made a plot and bound themselves by an oath neither to eat nor drink till they had killed Paul. ¹³There were more than forty who made this conspiracy. ¹⁴And they went to the chief priests and elders, and said, "We have strictly bound ourselves by an oath to taste no food till we have killed Paul. ¹⁵You therefore, along with the council, give notice now to the tribune to bring him down to you, as though you were going to determine his case more exactly. And we are ready to kill him before he comes near."

¹⁶Now the son of Paul's sister heard of their ambush; so he went and entered the barracks and told Paul. ¹⁷And Paul called one of the centurions and said, "Take this young man to the tribune; for he has something to tell him."

---

there, so now he **must bear witness** in **Rome** (for Rome as his destination, see notes on 19:21; for witnessing, see notes on 1:8).

[12-14] The rage and anger of the Jewish opponents had become white-hot. They took **an oath** in God's sight to kill Paul. Their conviction was manifest in that they were bound **neither to eat nor drink** until their oath was fulfilled. It is doubtful if these Jews starved, since Jewish tradition allowed a vow to remain unfulfilled if uncontrollable circumstances prevailed. **The chief priests** and **elders** were accomplices in this matter since they were told of the conspiracy.

[15] The complicity of **the council** was manifest in their eagerness to cooperate in Paul's assassination. Their part was to lure him out of the protection of the barracks. They were to give notice to the **tribune** that they wanted a retrial or at least the opportunity **to determine his case more exactly.** The forty conspirators, with Paul in the open, would kill him before he reached the Sanhedrin.

[16, 17] **The son of Paul's sister** is suddenly introduced. This is one of the few facts in the New Testament about Paul's family. Either members of Paul's family were still unbelieving Jews involved in the persecution of the Way, as

¹⁸So he took him and brought him to the tribune and said, "Paul the prisoner called me and asked me to bring this young man to you, as he has something to say to you." ¹⁹The tribune took him by the hand, and going aside asked him privately, "What is it that you have to tell me?" ²⁰And he said, "The Jews have agreed to ask you to bring Paul down to the council tomorrow, as though they were going to inquire somewhat more closely about him. ²¹But do not yield to them; for more than forty of their men lie in ambush for him, having bound themselves by an oath neither to eat nor drink till they have killed him; and now they are ready, waiting for the promise from you." ²²So the tribune dismissed the young man, charging him, "Tell no one that you have informed me of this."

²³Then he called two of the centurions and said, "At the third hour of the night get ready two hundred soldiers with seventy horsemen and two hundred spearmen to go as far as Caesarea. ²⁴Also provide mounts for Paul to ride, and bring him safely to Felix the governor."

Paul earlier had been, or this shows again the close ties still maintained between Jewish Christians and unbelieving Jews. The apostle's nephew **entered the barracks** and reported the plot to Paul. Paul had already shown that his policy was to flee whenever possible (cf. Matt. 10:23).

[18, 19] His nephew was instructed to report the scheme **to the tribune**, who was sworn to protect Roman citizens. Due to the explosiveness of the situation the matter was brought before the **tribune privately**.

[20-22] The **young man** rehearsed the plot to the Roman official. Perceiving the gravity of the situation, the **tribune dismissed** Paul's nephew with the charge to **tell no one**.

PAUL HELD AT CAESAREA, 23:23–26:32

Paul Sent to Felix, 23:23-35

[23, 24] Claudius Lysias recognized that the situation had developed into a crisis which exceeded his capabilities.

²⁵ And he wrote a letter to this effect:

²⁶ "Claudius Lysias to his Excellency the governor Felix, greeting. ²⁷ This man was seized by the Jews, and was about to be killed by them, when I came upon them with the soldiers and rescued him, having learned that he was a Roman citizen. ²⁸ And desiring to know the charge on which they accused him, I brought him down to their council. ²⁹ I found that he was accused about questions of their law, but charged with nothing deserving death or imprisonment. ³⁰ And when it was disclosed to me that there would be a plot against the man, I sent him to you at once, ordering his accusers also to state before you what they have against him."

Not desiring to be responsible for an assassinated prisoner, he judiciously sent Paul under armed guard to the **governor** (*hēgemōn*, cf. Matt. 10:18; 27:2; Mark 13:9; Luke 20:20; 21:12; Acts 24:1; 26:30; 1 Peter 2:14). **Caesarea**, a city still providing archeological results, was the residence of **Felix**. Our main sources, namely, Acts, Josephus, and Tacitus, paint a picture of irresponsible mismanagement, callousness, and corruption in regard to **Felix**. He became governor in A.D. 52 and was finally recalled by Rome in A.D. 59, not, however, before he had helped set into motion forces that eventually (in A.D. 66) precipitated the Jewish War (Josephus, *War* II.xii.8ff.; *Antiquities* XX.vii.1ff.; Tacitus, *Annals* 12.54; *Histories* 5.9).

A nocturnal departure, as well as the armed escort of **two hundred soldiers, seventy horsemen, and two hundred spearmen**, guaranteed the apostle's safety.

[25-30] These verses contain a letter based upon Luke's knowledge of the events which demanded Paul's removal to Caesarea. Since he had no access to the letter personally, he states that Claudius' **letter** was **to this effect** (Greek, having this form or content).

Basically **Lysias'** letter retold the events of Acts 21:27–23:22. One prominent mistake in his letter, surely put there to ingratiate **Felix**, was the statement that the tribune

[31] So the soldiers, according to their instructions, took Paul and brought him by night to Antipatris. [32] And on the morrow they returned to the barracks, leaving the horsemen to go on with him. [33] When they came to Caesarea and delivered the letter to the governor, they presented Paul also before him. [34] On reading the letter, he asked to what province he belonged. When he learned that he was from Cilicia [35] he said, "I will hear you when your accusers arrive." And he commanded him to be guarded in Herod's praetorium.

---

rescued Paul when he had learned that Paul **was a Roman citizen**. The Jewish **accusers** were informed about this unannounced change of venue after Paul was safely out of their reach. Significantly the tribune passed on to his superior his own judgment (not presented earlier) that Paul was guilty of **nothing deserving death or imprisonment**.

[31-35] Their night journey of approximately forty miles brought them to **Antipatris**. This city, rebuilt by Herod the Great and named after his father Antipater, procurator of Judea under Julius Caesar, was a military station and demarcation between Samaria and Judea. **On the morrow** most of the armed guard **returned to the barracks** while the others continued the remaining twenty miles or so to **Caesarea**.

Felix inquired concerning the **province** to which Paul **belonged** (cf. Luke 23:6). In Roman law it was optional whether an individual had to be tried in his home province. Moreover, since Tarsus was a free state, its citizens were exempt from provincial jurisdiction. It is also a question whether **Cilicia** at this point in time was a legal province or under the judicial control of the legate of Syria.

Felix decided to **hear** the case (*diakouō*, a technical term in ancient jurisprudence) when Paul's **accusers** arrived. Meanwhile Paul was guarded **in Herod's praetorium** (cf. Matt. 27:27; Mark 15:16; John 18:28; 19:9; Phil. 1:13). The **praetorium** was a palace built by **Herod** the Great which now served as official residence of the **governor**.

¹**And after five days the high priest Ananias came down
with some elders and a spokesman, one Tertullus. They laid
before the governor their case against Paul;** ²**and when he was
called, Tertullus began to accuse him, saying:**

**"Since through you we enjoy much peace, and since by
your provision, most excellent Felix, reforms are introduced
on behalf of this nation,** ³**in every way and everywhere we
accept this with all gratitude.** ⁴**But, to detain you no further, I
beg you in your kindness to hear us briefly.** ⁵**For we have
found this man a pestilent fellow, an agitator among all the
Jews throughout the world, and a ringleader of the sect of the
Nazarenes.**

The Jews' Case Against Paul, 24:1-9

[1] The **five days** provided Paul's accusers a period to
recover after learning that their prey had fled and their oath
(23:12-15) was in vain. Luke employed the word *rhētōr* to
describe **Tertullus**. This term usually signified an orator, but
in legal context it meant an attorney.

[2, 3] Adulation characterized Tertullus' opening remarks to **Felix**. Since the case was laid before the governor
and not a council, this type of flattery was commonplace.
Words such as **peace, reforms, gratitude,** and **kindness** were
hardly commensurate with an incompetent official recalled
by Rome and spared, then, only by nepotistic connections
in the capital city. True, **Felix** had executed numerous
religious freedom fighters (Josephus, *War* II. 253-263), but
many Jews would have suggested that peace was in spite of
Felix's policies and not because of his irenic character.
Provision (*pronoia*, care or providence) and **kindness** hardly
seemed appropriate epithets for a man described by Tacitus,
the Roman historian, with the statement "He indulged in
every kind of savagery and passion, exercizing the power of
a king with the disposition of a slave" (*Histories* 5.9).

[4, 5] In traditional form, **Tertullus** promised to state his
case **briefly**.

The first accusation against Paul was that he was a

⁶**He even tried to profane the temple, but we seized him.**ᶻ

ᶻ Other ancient authorities add *and we would have judged him according to our law.* ⁷*But the chief captain Lysias came and with great violence took him out of our hands,* ⁸*commanding his accusers to come before you.*

---

pestilent fellow. Tertullus' exact word *loimos* is more pregnant with meaning than most commentaries note. *Loimos* denoted a plague and was metaphorically applied to people considered a threat to society—like the plague. What is often overlooked in regard to this verse is the other times this derisive concept was used against Christians in antiquity. In the Pliny-Trajan *Letters* (10.96.9) Pliny pictured Christian evangelism as a disease infecting (*contagio pervagata est*) the countryside (cf. Tacitus, *Annals* 15.44). In an official letter written in A.D. 41 to Alexandrian Jews and pagans, the Emperor Claudius mentioned Jewish troublemakers from Syria who had come to Egypt. He reckoned them as fomentors of a general plague (*loimos*) that was infecting the whole world. He may well have been referring to Jewish Christians from the Syrian city of Antioch.

The apostle was next charged with being an **agitator among all the Jews.** Even a cursory reading of Acts leaves little doubt about the accuracy of this statement (see notes on Acts 19:40, 41 and Suetonius, *Claudius* 25.4). Then the prosecutor for the Jews labeled the believers a **sect of the Nazarenes.** The term **sect** (*hairesis*) could refer to a particular party or school within a philosophy (e.g., Stoics) or the various branches of Jewish thought (Sadducees, Acts 5:17; Josephus, *Antiquities* XIII.171; Pharisees, Acts 15:5). Tertullus used this term in a negative sense, which displeased Paul (24:14; cf. 28:22). This is the only instance in early Christian literature of believers being called **sect of the Nazarenes,** probably because of its Palestinian color.

[6] The third charge was that Paul **tried to profane** (*bebēloō*, Ezek. 20:13c; 28:18; Matt. 12:5) **the temple** (cf. Acts 6:13; 21:28).

149

⁸ By examining him yourself you will be able to learn from him about everything of which we accuse him."

⁹ The Jews also joined in the charge, affirming that all this was so.

¹⁰ And when the governor had motioned to him to speak, Paul replied:

"Realizing that for many years you have been judge over this nation, I cheerfully make my defense. ¹¹ As you may ascertain, it is not more than twelve days since I went up to worship at Jerusalem; ¹² and they did not find me disputing with any one or stirring up a crowd, either in the temple or in the synagogues, or in the city. ¹³ Neither can they prove to you what they now bring up against me. ¹⁴ But this I admit to you, that according to the Way, which they call a sect, I worship the God of our fathers, believing everything laid down by the law or written in the prophets, ¹⁵ having a hope in God which these themselves accept, that there will be a resurrection of both the just and the unjust. ¹⁶ So I always take pains to have a clear conscience toward God and toward men.

[8, 9] Tertullus rested his case, confident that by **examining** Paul Felix would take the side of the **Jews**.

Paul's Defense before Felix, 24:10-21

[10-13] Paul judiciously began his defense (*apologeomai*) by refuting the charges leveled against him. He had been away from **Jerusalem** for **years**, and **twelve days** (five of which he had spent in custody since his arrest, so 24:1) was hardly time to be as pestiferous as Tertullus charged. Paul stated his case: he was not **disputing** in the temple or **stirring up a crowd**. He placed the burden of proof on those who asserted otherwise.

[14-16] Since Felix had been judge over Israel many years (24:10), he knew the wranglings and abstruse legalism which often characterized Jewish infighting. The apostle's strategy here was based upon his experience at Corinth. He must shift the argument from political to religious matters.

[17] Now after some years I came to bring to my nation alms and offerings. [18] As I was doing this, they found me purified in the temple, without any crowd or tumult. But some Jews from Asia—[19] they ought to be here before you and to make an accusation, if they have anything against me. [20] Or else let these men themselves say what wrongdoing they found when I stood before the council, [21] except this one thing which I cried out while standing among them, 'With respect to the resurrection of the dead I am on trial before you this day.' "

Consequently Paul was eager to admit the nature of his religious beliefs. He (1) worshiped the Jewish **God**, (2) believed everything in the **law** and **the prophets** (the Jewish Bible), and (3) held to the Jewish **hope in God**—the **resurrection of both the just and the unjust** (see notes on 23:6). Since judgment was connected with Paul's conception of the resurrection and salvation, he always took pains to have a **clear conscience** (see notes on 23:1).

[**17-21**] He finished his defense with his own reconstruction of what transpired. **Some years** indicated the time between Acts 18:22 (greeted the church) and 21:17. Clearly the Jerusalem **offering** did not figure as prominently in Acts as in Paul's letters. Nevertheless, it is assumed by the narrative in Acts 20:4-6 (see notes there) and prominent in Paul's rationale for his trip to the holy city. Paul was **purified** (cf. 21:24, 26) and unobtrusive when **Jews from Asia** attacked him.

Remembering that the burden of proof lay with his detractors, Paul abruptly stopped his defense. **They**, Paul asserted, **ought to be** present making accusations since the high priest and elders were not present in the temple at the time of the alleged crime and wrongdoing. Regarding the temple incident Ananias and the elders could only offer hearsay testimony. They could only testify to possible **wrongdoing** committed by Paul when he stood **before the council** (cf. 23:6). Paul rested his case, having temporarily discredited the case brought against him by the Jews.

²²**But Felix, having a rather accurate knowledge of the Way, put them off, saying, "When Lysias the tribune comes down, I will decide your case."** ²³**Then he gave orders to the centurion that he should be kept in custody but should have some liberty, and that none of his friends should be prevented from attending to his needs.**

²⁴**After some days Felix came with his wife Drusilla, who was a Jewess; and he sent for Paul and heard him speak upon faith in Christ Jesus.**

Delayed Judgment, 24:22, 23

[22] Luke notes that Felix's **knowlege of the Way** (cf. 19:9) was **rather accurate** (cf. 18:25, 26). Therefore, he felt comfortable in withholding his verdict until further testimony could be taken. Felix's quandary about the disposition of Paul's case was typical of Roman officials. Their own personal knowledge of Christianity would lead them to a neutral position. However, once someone brought a charge against a Christian, then the governor had to take some form of action (see esp. *Letters* of Pliny 10.96, 97).

[23] The ruling of Felix was to keep Paul under a type of house arrest. He was **in custody**, but with **some liberty** (cf. 27:3; 28:16, 30) and accessible to all of **his friends** who might attend **his needs**. Luke's reference to Paul's lengthy imprisonment furnishes us a glimpse into the life situation of the primitive church. Here is a typical context for the numerous verses of scripture which allude to visiting and ministering to the needs of imprisoned believers (Matt. 25:43, 44; Phil. 2:25; Phile. 13; Heb. 10:34; 13:3).

Reasoning with Felix and Drusilla, 24:24-27

[24] The fact that Felix's **wife** was Jewish certainly increased his knowledge of Judaism and its various components. This **Drusilla** was the younger sister of Herod Agrippa II and Bernice (Acts 25:13). The apostle was summoned to speak on **faith in Christ Jesus**.

²⁵ **And as he argued about justice and self-control and future judgment, Felix was alarmed and said, "Go away for the present; when I have an opportunity I will summon you."** ²⁶ **At the same time he hoped that money would be given him by Paul. So he sent for him often and conversed with him.** ²⁷ **But when two years had elapsed, Felix was succeeded by Porcius Festus; and desiring to do the Jews a favor, Felix left Paul in prison.**

¹ **Now when Festus had come into his province, after three days he went up to Jerusalem from Caesarea.**

---

[25] Paul preached about **justice** (*dikaiosunē*), **self-control** (*enkrateia*; cf. 1 Cor. 7:9; 9:25; Gal. 5:23; Titus 1:8; 2 Peter 1:6), and **future judgment** (see 17:31 and notes there). One with Felix's tendency to immorality and corruption should have been **alarmed** as Paul argued. He sent the apostle **away**, no longer able to hear such **judgment**.

[26] Luke's words about the governor's fear is an example par excellence of Paul's description of "worldly grief" (2 Cor. 7:10). Had Felix and Drusilla experienced a godly grief, repentance would have come forth. As it was, Felix **hoped** for **money** from the prisoner to purchase a favorable judgment (cf. 24:17).

[27] **Two years** later **Felix** was recalled to Rome. Much conversation but no money passed from Paul to **Felix**. Moreover, **Felix** hoped to placate the **Jews** since they were the ones prosecuting him at Rome for corruption. Perhaps, he reasoned, he could win **favor** with the **Jews** by leaving **Paul in prison** and thereby assuage their wrath at his inept rule.

The Jews and Festus, 25:1-5

[1] Porcius **Festus** replaced Felix as governor. He surpassed Felix in administrative ability and wisdom. Unfortunately, his tenure of office was much shorter, lasting only A.D. 60–62 (some date his term A.D. 56–58).

153

²And the chief priests and the principal men of the Jews informed him against Paul; and they urged him, ³asking as a favor to have the man sent to Jerusalem, planning an ambush to kill him on the way. ⁴Festus replied that Paul was being kept at Caesarea, and that he himself intended to go there shortly. ⁵"So," said he, "let the men of authority among you go down with me, and if there is anything wrong about the man, let them accuse him."

⁶When he had stayed among them not more than eight or ten days, he went down to Caesarea; and the next day he took his seat on the tribunal and ordered Paul to be brought.

In a gesture of administrative propriety **Festus, after** only **three days** at **Caesarea**, went up to consult with the **Jerusalem** hierarchy. The political situation in Palestine was quite volatile, and he needed to dispel as many fears as he could in the minds of the wary guardians of Judaism.

[2, 3] During their discussions the issue of Paul was brought up by the **chief priests** and **principal men** (Sanhedrin). They seized the opportunity to reactivate their assassination plot. Hoping to find Festus in a courteous frame of mind, they urged him **as a favor** to return Paul **to Jerusalem** for retrial. One does not know whether this new governor suspected their motives.

[4, 5] They were not able to inveigle **Festus**. Paul was a Roman prisoner and would remain at Herod's praetorium (23:35). Jewish **men of authority** could follow proper channels. If there was a **wrong, let them accuse him**, for that was the way of Roman jurisprudence (Pliny, *Letters* 10.97.2; for charges against believers see Acts 22:30; 23:29, 30; 24:2, 8, 13; 25:5, 11, 16, 18; 26:2, 7; 1 Peter 2:12; 3:15, 16).

Paul before Festus, 25:6-12

[6] After a stay of less than a fortnight Festus returned **to Caesarea** and brought Paul out to appear before the imperial **tribunal** (*bēma*, cf. notes on 18:12b), thus indicating court was in session.

⁷And when he had come, the Jews who had gone down from Jerusalem stood about him, bringing against him many serious charges which they could not prove. ⁸Paul said in his defense, "Neither against the law of the Jews, nor against the temple, nor against Caesar have I offended at all." ⁹But Festus, wishing to do the Jews a favor, said to Paul, "Do you wish to go up to Jerusalem, and there be tried on these charges before me?" ¹⁰But Paul said, "I am standing before Caesar's tribunal, where I ought to be tried; to the Jews I have done no wrong, as you know very well. ¹¹If then I am a wrongdoer, and have committed anything for which I deserve to die, I do not seek to escape death; but if there is nothing in their charges against me, no one can give me up to them. I appeal to Caesar." ¹²Then Festus, when he had conferred with his council, answered, "You have appealed to Caesar; to Caesar you shall go."

[7, 8] The Jews faced Paul once again in a legal context (cf. Acts 17:6-9; 18:12-14; 23:1-10; 24:1-9), bringing **serious charges**. The apostle denied three charges, all of which were serious: offense **against the law of the Jews**, threats **against the temple**, and acting **against** the decrees of **Caesar**.

[9-12] The political reality of administrating such a volatile region as Palestine included ingratiating oneself with the provincials. In Luke's words, Festus wanted **to do the Jews a favor**. Festus tried to convince **Paul** to return **to Jerusalem** for trial. Since that was tantamount to suicide, **Paul** reminded Festus that he was under Roman, not Jewish, custody and law. The apostle bore in his body the scars of Jewish wrath and persecution. On this occasion, however, he refused to be given **up to** their style of justice. Totally to preclude this possibility he appealed **to Caesar**. With this appeal he began an inexorable course to Rome, a course already assigned to him by the Lord (19:21; 23:11; 27:24).

Earlier (22:24-29 and notes there) Paul the Roman citizen used his citizenship to eliminate an imminent scourging. A second privilege of citizenship was that the citizen had the

¹³ Now when some days had passed, **Agrippa the king and Bernice arrived at Caesarea to welcome Festus.** ¹⁴ **And as they stayed there many days, Festus laid Paul's case before the king, saying, "There is a man left prisoner by Felix;** ¹⁵ **and when I was at Jerusalem, the chief priests and the elders of the Jews gave information about him, asking for sentence against him.** ¹⁶ **I answered them that it was not the custom of the Romans to give up any one before the accused met the accusers face to face, and had opportunity to make his defense concerning the charge laid against him.**

---

right to **appeal to Caesar** himself for justice in capital cases (as Paul's was, 25:11). The Pliny-Trajan *Letters* of the early second century record a similar situation in which Christian provincials who were Roman citizens were sent to Rome for trial (*Letters* 10. 96.3, 4).

Agrippa and Bernice's Visit, 25:13-27

[13] **Agrippa the king** is a shortened form of the full name Herod Agrippa II. Herod the Great (Matt. 2:1; Luke 1:5) had ten wives and, understandably, an extensive progeny. Herod **Agrippa** II (ca. A.D. 30–100) was the last of the Herodian line, being the son of Herod **Agrippa** I (Acts 12:1-23) and a great grandson of Herod the Great. As the flames of the Jewish revolt were fanned in the ensuing years, both **Agrippa** and **Bernice**, his sister, sided with Rome. In fact, **Bernice** later became the mistress of Titus, the conqueror of Jerusalem (Josephus, *War* II.xi.6; *Antiquities* XIX.v.1; Tacitus, *Histories* 2.2).

[14, 15] **Festus** laid Paul's case before Agrippa and Bernice. Most of this section is a summary of Acts 25:7-12, but the author gives some information that was not mentioned in the previous account.

[16] The governor acknowledged a **custom** (*ethos*) **of the Romans** on which Paul earlier relied; namely, **the accused** has the right to meet **the accusers face to face** (24:19, 20; cf. Appian, *Civil War* 3.54).

[17] When therefore they came together here, I made no delay, but on the next day took my seat on the tribunal and ordered the man to be brought in. [18] When the accusers stood up, they brought no charge in his case of such evils as I supposed; [19] but they had certain points of dispute with him about their own superstition and about one Jesus, who was dead, but whom Paul asserted to be alive. [20] Being at a loss how to investigate these questions, I asked whether he wished to go to Jerusalem and be tried there regarding them. [21] But when Paul had appealed to be kept in custody for the decision of the emperor, I commanded him to be held until I could send him to Caesar." [22] And Agrippa said to Festus, "I should like to hear the man myself." "Tomorrow," said he, "you shall hear him."

[23] So on the morrow Agrippa and Bernice came with great pomp, and they entered the audience hall with the military tribunes and the prominent men of the city. Then by command of Festus Paul was brought in.

[17-20] Festus continued his narration observing that the Jews **came** and **brought** charges. But **no charge** was as serious as he had anticipated. What he had learned, as his fellow Roman Gallio had earlier learned, was that the Jewish antagonism against believers in **Jesus** was of a religious nature and not a legal matter, at least not legal in the sphere of Roman law. Notwithstanding the legal confusion that accompanied these sessions, Festus heard with singular clarity that the issue was **Jesus**, once **dead** but now **alive** (see Acts 17:18, 31; 23:6; 24:21; 28:20).

Festus was **at a loss** because his administrative expertise did not cover such **questions**. He suggested that the problem be passed on and resolved elsewhere.

[21, 22] The governor's report ended with Paul's decision to see **Caesar**. **Agrippa** then expressed his desire **to hear** Paul himself.

[23] The **great pomp** linked here with **Agrippa and Bernice** brings to mind the regalia in which their father

²⁴And Festus said, "King Agrippa and all who are present with us, you see this man about whom the whole Jewish people petitioned me, both at Jerusalem and here, shouting that he ought not to live any longer. ²⁵But I found that he had done nothing deserving death; and as he himself appealed to the emperor, I decided to send him. ²⁶But I have nothing definite to write to my lord about him. Therefore I have brought him before you, and, especially before you, King Agrippa, that, after we have examined him, I may have something to write. ²⁷For it seems to me unreasonable, in sending a prisoner, not to indicate the charges against him."

¹Agrippa said to Paul, "You have permission to speak for yourself." Then Paul stretched out his hand and made his defense:

Agrippa I appeared the day he died (Acts 12:21). The **audience hall** was the place for Paul's hearing. This was not an official trial. Rather, it was conducted as a favor for **Agrippa** to satisfy his curiosity and perhaps that of the city's **prominent men**.

[24-27] The content of these verses is well known to the reader. They were given by Luke to afford another chance to demonstrate with an apologetic thrust Paul's vindication by Roman law. Thus it is mentioned that the Jews shouted for Paul's death though he **had done nothing deserving death**. Furthermore, Roman officials were in the almost burlesque position of having a Roman **prisoner** against whom they had no **charges**. Festus perhaps implied a judgment on the Jews when he characterized the whole situation as **unreasonable**.

Paul's Address to Agrippa, 26:1-32

Introduction, 26:1-3. [1] When **Paul** was granted permission to speak, he began his defense (*apologeomai*). This is his second apologetic account of his conversion recorded by Luke (cf. 22:1ff.).

² "I think myself fortunate that it is before you, King Agrippa, I am to make my defense today against all the accusations of the Jews, ³ because you are especially familiar with all customs and controversies of the Jews; therefore I beg you to listen to me patiently.

⁴ "My manner of life from my youth, spent from the beginning among my own nation and at Jerusalem, is known by all the Jews. ⁵ They have known for a long time, if they are willing to testify, that according to the strictest party of our religion I have lived as a Pharisee. ⁶ And now I stand here on trial for hope in the promise made by God to our fathers, ⁷ to which our twelve tribes hope to attain, as they earnestly worship night and day. And for this hope I am accused by Jews, O king! ⁸ Why is it thought incredible by any of you that God raises the dead?

[2, 3] Since **King Agrippa** was **especially familiar** with Jewish **customs** (*ethos*) and sectarian differences, Paul considered himself **fortunate** to stand **before** him.

Paul's Life as a Jew, 26:4-11. [4, 5] The orthodoxy of the apostle's **life** and education was stressed by the expressions **among my own nation**, **at Jerusalem**, and **strictest party of our religion**. The clear intent of these points was to show that Paul could hardly be the religious rabble-rouser he was accused of being (cf. Gal. 1:14; Phil. 3:5, 6).

[6-8] From his first defense before the Jerusalem hierarchy (22:6) Paul focused attention on the issue of resurrection (cf. Acts 13:30-37) rather than on issues such as faith versus works of the law (13:39) or the Gentile mission (22:21). The motif of **hope** (*elpis*) has previously appeared in Acts related to the resurrection (2:26; 23:6; 24:15; 26:7; 28:20; cf. 1 Cor. 15:19).

Paul stressed that this **hope** was in the patriarchal **promise** given **by God**. Promise (*epaggelia*) was understood variously in New Testament writings. The **promise of God** was frequently the Holy Spirit (Luke 24:49; Acts 1:4; 2:33, 39; Gal. 3:14; Eph. 1:13), the Parousia of Christ

159

⁹"I myself was convinced that I ought to do many things in opposing the name of Jesus of Nazareth. ¹⁰And I did so in Jerusalem; I not only shut up many of the saints in prison, by authority from the chief priests, but when they were put to death I cast my vote against them. ¹¹And I punished them often in all the synagogues and tried to make them blaspheme; and in raging fury against them, I persecuted them even to foreign cities.

¹²"Thus I journeyed to Damascus with the authority and commission of the chief priests. ¹³At midday, O king, I saw on the way a light from heaven, brighter than the sun, shining round me and those who journeyed with me. ¹⁴And when we had all fallen to the ground, I heard a voice saying to me in the Hebrew language, 'Saul, Saul, why do you persecute me? It hurts you to kick against the goads.'

(2 Peter 3:4; cf. 1 John 2:25), and the resurrection of Jesus (Acts 13:23, 32; 26:6). The relationship between the patriarchs and the resurrection was discussed by Jesus (Matt. 22:31, 32; Mark 12:26; Luke 20:37, 38). It was ironic that Paul was **accused by the Jews** when it was their very **hope** for which he struggled.

The apostle's reference to skepticism **that God** can raise **the dead** demonstrated a view similar to that of 1 Corinthians 15:12-19. One cannot dissociate belief in Jesus' resurrection from belief in the general resurrection, and vice versa.

[9-11] These verses retell the apostle's pre-Christian attacks against **the name of Jesus of Nazareth** (see notes on 22:4, 5; cf. Acts 8:1-3; 9:1, 2). When Saul punished Christians **in all the synagogues** and **persecuted them even to foreign cities**, little did he realize how accurately this described what the Jews would later do to him.

Appearance of Jesus, 26:12-18. [12-18] Though this account is much like the previous ones (see notes on 9:3, 4; 22:6, 7), two items are mentioned only here. On this occasion the speaker reported that the address **Saul, Saul** was

¹⁵And I said, 'Who are you, Lord?' And the Lord said, 'I am Jesus whom you are persecuting. ¹⁶But rise and stand upon your feet; for I have appeared to you for this purpose, to appoint you to serve and bear witness to the things in which you have seen me and to those in which I will appear to you, ¹⁷delivering you from the people and from the Gentiles—to whom I send you ¹⁸to open their eyes, that they may turn from darkness to light and from the power of Satan to God, that they may receive forgiveness of sins and a place among those who are sanctified by faith in me.'

---

spoken **in the Hebrew language** (Aramaic; cf. 21:40). The proverbial epigram **it hurts you to kick against the goads**, preserved only here, is extant in Latin and Greek secular writings of antiquity (e.g., Aeschylus, *Agamemnon* 1624; Euripides, *Bacchae* 795). This type of statement would be at home in any agrarian context, since the imagery of kicking **against the goad** was that of a balking animal kicking against an unyielding stick or **goad**.

Luke here presents an abbreviated account of Paul's confrontation with the Lord; for example, there is no mention of blindness or Ananias' mission. The call and commissioning of the prophet Ezekiel are brought to mind (Ezek. 1:28–2:7; cf. Jer. 1:7), with Paul's use of the expressions: **light from heaven brighter than the sun** (Ezek. 1:28a); **fallen to the ground I heard a voice** (Ezek. 1:28b); **stand upon your feet** (Ezek. 2:1); **to whom I send you** (Ezek. 2:4); and **bear witness** (Ezek. 2:2-7).

Luke emphasizes here the close relationship of Jesus' appearance to Paul and his apostolic commission (26:16b), a perspective also stressed in Paul's own writings (1 Cor. 9:1; cf. 1 Cor. 15:8). The apostle's revelations from and of Christ did not end here. He also bore **witness** to ideas and events which were revealed to him at later times.

The brief description of Paul's message in Acts 26:18 is replete with doctrinal motifs found in his letters (see especially Col. 1:13, 14; Eph. 2:2).

¹⁹ "Wherefore, O King Agrippa, I was not disobedient to the heavenly vision, ²⁰ but declared first to those at Damascus, then at Jerusalem and throughout all the country of Judea, and also to the Gentiles, that they should repent and turn to God and perform deeds worthy of their repentance. ²¹ For this reason the Jews seized me in the temple and tried to kill me. ²² To this day I have had the help that comes from God, and so I stand here testifying both to small and great, saying nothing but what the prophets and Moses said would come to pass: ²³ that the Christ must suffer, and that, by being the first to rise from the dead, he would proclaim light both to the people and to the Gentiles."

Paul's Obedience, 26:19-23. [19, 20] Paul emphatically declared his obedience **to the heavenly vision** and subsequent proclamation **to those in Damascus** (cf. Acts 9:19-27; 2 Cor. 11:32; Gal. 1:17), **then at Jerusalem** and in **Judea** (cf. Gal. 1:18). Inherent in the repentance of **the Gentiles** was a turning **to God** (cf. 1 Thess. 1:9; also Acts 9:35; 14:15; 15:19 for this idiom). The word **repentance**, while frequent in the preaching of Jesus and the early church, appears infrequently in the Pauline letters (cf. Rom. 2:4; 2 Cor. 7:9, 10; 2 Tim. 2:25). However, the concept of **deeds** or works (*erga*) which are necessarily predicated on salvation and **repentance** was central to Paul's religious teachings (e.g., Eph. 2:10 and notes on Acts 20:32) as was the concept of commensurate (= **worthy**, *axios*) performance (Eph. 4:1; Phil. 1:27; Col. 1:10; 1 Thess. 2:12; cf. 1 Cor. 11:27).

[21-23] For this reason meant the Gentile mission which indirectly led to his initial imprisonment (Acts 21:28). God's abiding **help** had enabled his servant to **stand** before **great and small**. He appealed next to Jesus' fulfillment of the prophetic teaching of **Moses** and the other prophets. Specifically this was the suffering, death, and resurrection of the **Christ** (cf. Luke 24:27, 44). It would be difficult to find a single statement which better recapitulated the core of Paul's gospel.

²⁴And as he thus made his defense, Festus said with a loud voice, "Paul, you are mad; your great learning is turning you mad." ²⁵But Paul said, "I am not mad, most excellent Festus, but I am speaking the sober truth. ²⁶For the king knows about these things, and to him I speak freely; for I am persuaded that none of these things has escaped his notice, for this was not done in a corner. ²⁷King Agrippa, do you believe the prophets? I know that you believe." ²⁸And Agrippa said to Paul, "In a short time you think to make me a Christian!"

Jewish history and the Gospels clearly demonstrate that Jesus was not thought to be **the first** to be brought back to life after death (e.g., 1 Kings 17:23; 2 Kings 4:32-37; 13:21; John 11:38-44; Heb. 11:35). Paul's statement **by being the first to rise from the dead** referred to the concept of Christ being the first fruits of the dead (1 Cor. 15:20, 23; Col. 1:18). The dual mission, **to the people** (*laos*) or Jews (see on 15:14) and **to the Gentiles**, meant Christ's proclamation through his apostolic servants. The term **light** (*phōs*) was sometimes a catchword in Luke for the universality of God's message based upon Old Testament servant concepts (e.g., Isa. 49:6). This particular use of the **light** motif is recorded in Luke 2:32; Acts 13:47; 26:23 (see notes on Acts 13:47).

Response to Paul's Address, 26:24-32. [24, 25] Luke has already prepared the reader for Festus' ridicule of the Christian gospel (see 25:19, 20; cf. 26:8). The governor exclaimed in **a loud voice** that **Paul** had gone **mad** (*mainomai*). This term was much stronger than the idea that the gospel and its bearers were merely foolish (e.g., 1 Cor. 1:25, 27; 3:18; 4:10). This charge by **Festus** was closer to an accusation of lunacy (see John 10:20; Acts 12:15; 1 Cor. 14:23 for use of this term; cf. Acts 17:32).

[26-28] Confronted with such a sharp rebuttal from Festus, Paul turned to **King** Agrippa for support and agreement. Since the events of Christianity were not conducted **in a corner**, the **king** could attest the apostle's truthfulness. Moreover the **king** believed **the prophets**, the second pillar

163

²⁹ And Paul said, "Whether short or long, I would to God that not only you but also all who hear me this day might become such as I am—except for these chains."

³⁰ Then the king rose, and the governor and Bernice and those who were sitting with them; ³¹ and when they had withdrawn, they said to one another, "This man is doing nothing to deserve death or imprisonment." ³² And Agrippa said to Festus, "This man could have been set free if he had not appealed to Caesar."

¹ And when it was decided that we should sail for Italy, they delivered Paul and some other prisoners to a centurion of the Augustan Cohort, named Julius.

---

on which the message rested. Paul found little sympathy in Herod **Agrippa** II. The **king** with sarcasm in his voice retorted that Paul was not going to convert him to Christianity that quickly. This is the second instance of the word **Christian** (*Christianos*) in Acts (cf. 11:26).

[29] Paul concluded with an evangelistic plea that **all who** heard him **would** become what he was, namely, a Christian.

[30-32] After the audience was over, Festus, Agrippa, and Bernice spoke to one another and concluded that though the prisoner might be mad or overly zealous, he was **doing nothing to deserve death** or **imprisonment**. With all proper means of inquiry and litigation exhausted and both the governor and the king satisfied, the natural question became why is not **this man set free**. The answer came in Agrippa's comment that **if** Paul **had not appealed** to the emperor he could now have been released. This may or may not imply that the Sanhedrin had been placated or at least given up on their litigation against Paul.

PAUL'S JOURNEY TO ROME, 27:1–28:16

Sailing to Crete, 27:1-12

[1] The term **sail** (*apopleō*; cf. Acts 13:4; 14:26; 20:15)

²And embarking in a ship of Adramyttium, which was about to sail to the ports along the coast of Asia, we put to sea, accompanied by Aristarchus, a Macedonian from Thessalonica. ³The next day we put in at Sidon; and Julius treated Paul kindly, and gave him leave to go to his friends and be cared for. ⁴And putting to sea from there we sailed under the lee of Cyprus, because the winds were against us. ⁵And when we had sailed across the sea which is off Cilicia and Pamphylia, we came to Myra in Lycia. ⁶There the centurion found a ship of Alexandria sailing for Italy, and put us on board.

---

sets the tone for the next section of Acts. In Acts 27:1–28:16 is some of the most vivid narrative, as well as most technical and difficult Greek, in the book of Acts. As the **we** proves, this account was a reliable, firsthand, eyewitness record of what transpired (see Introduction, part 1, pp. 8, 11).This detailed report of navigational matters abounds with technical and often disputed terminology and allusions. Most of these technical concerns do not fall within the purview of this commentary. However, the interested student can still profit greatly from consultation of James Smith, *The Voyage and Shipwreck of St. Paul* (fourth edition, 1880; reprinted 1978 by Baker Book House, Grand Rapids). The style and content of this Lukan narrative rank it with similar accounts from the Graeco-Roman times (e.g., Lucian, *The Ship* 5-9).

A certain **Julius, a centurion of the Augustan Cohort** (attested by Latin inscriptions) was given charge of Paul. A cohort was usually the tenth part of a legion of 6,000 soldiers.

[2] There were no direct ships to Italy, so they took a ship (probably at Caesarea) sailing for **Adramyttium** (northwest Turkey south of Assos and adjacent to Lesbos). Paul and Luke were accompanied by **Aristarchus** (cf. Acts 19:29; 20:4), who apparently only later was imprisoned (Col. 4:10; cf., however, Phile. 23, 24).

[3-6] These verses summarily describe the traveler's voyage along the coast of Palestine and then the southern

⁷We sailed slowly for a number of days, and arrived with difficulty off Cnidus, and as the wind did not allow us to go on, we sailed under the lee of Crete off Salmone. ⁸Coasting along it with difficulty, we came to a place called Fair Havens, near which was the city of Lasea.

⁹As much time had been lost, and the voyage was already dangerous because the fast had already gone by, Paul advised them,

---

coast of Turkey. In deference to Paul's citizenship he was allowed to disembark **at Sidon**. Commerce was probably the occasion for this stop, since Sidon was the metropolis of the Phoenicians (cf. Strabo, *Geography* 16.2.4). **At Sidon** Paul was **cared for** (cf. notes on Acts 16:5; 24:23) by **friends**, a term probably designating Christians (cf. John 15:14ff.; Luke 12:4; Acts 24:23; and especially 3 John 15).

Since the wind would have been against them had they **sailed** due west, they **sailed under the lee of Cyprus** on its eastward face. Following the southern littoral of Turkey they arrived at **Myra in Lycia**. At this juncture they transferred to another **ship**, this one enroute from **Alexandria** to **Italy**. This wheat **ship** (27:38) was part of a large commercial fleet (governmentally regulated) which regularly and frequently carried grain from Egypt (Rome's breadbasket) to **Italy**.

[7, 8] Their journey was difficult, and after they had passed through the waters between **Cnidus** and Rhodes the inopportune wind forced them to sail **under the lee of Crete**. With continued **difficulty** from the weather they coasted along the southern shore of **Crete** until they reached **Fair Havens**.

[9] Safe navigation on the Mediterranean was acutely seasonal. **Lost time** was precious. The Jewish liturgical calendar was assumed by Luke (cf. Acts 1:12; 12:4; 20:6, 16) when he observed that the **fast** (*nēsteia* = Day of Atonement) was **already gone**. Ancient writers reflected Luke's and Paul's concern when noting that travel in open

¹⁰saying, "Sirs, I perceive that the voyage will be with injury and much loss, not only of the cargo and the ship, but also of our lives." ¹¹But the centurion paid more attention to the captain and to the owner of the ship than to what Paul said. ¹²And because the harbor was not suitable to winter in, the majority advised to put to sea from there, on the chance that somehow they could reach Phoenix, a harbor of Crete, looking northeast and southeast,ᵃ and winter there.

¹³And when the south wind blew gently, supposing that they had obtained their purpose, they weighed anchor and sailed along Crete, close inshore. ¹⁴But soon a tempestuous wind, called the northeaster, struck down from the land; ¹⁵and when the ship was caught and could not face the wind, we gave way to it and were driven.

ᵃOr *southwest and northwest*

---

seas was dangerous after September 15 and virtually suicidal after November 11. The **fast** in that particular year, according to F. F. Bruce (*The Book of Acts*, p. 506), was in mid-October.

[10, 11] Paul warned them that **loss of life** and property awaited them if they continued on their **voyage**. The others decided not to winter at Fair Havens.

[12] Luke noted that **the harbor** in fact was not suitable for **winter** at least not as suitable as the Cretan **harbor** of **Phoenix**, which faced in a more propitious direction to protect a ship from **winter** storms.

Storm at Sea, 27:13-20

[13-15] A gentle **south wind** led them to believe that they could now safely make Phoenix. **They weighed anchor** and **sailed** cautiously **close** to the **shore**. This, however, was only the proverbial calm before the storm. A **tempestuous** (*tuphōnikos*, hence English *typhoon*) **wind** broke upon them (cf. Pliny, *Natural History* 2.132). This **northeaster caught the ship** and drove it southeasterly for about twenty-five miles to the leeward side of Cauda.

¹⁶**And running under the lee of a small island called Cauda,**ᵇ
we managed with difficulty to secure the boat; ¹⁷**after hoisting
it up, they took measures**ᶜ **to undergird the ship; then, fearing
that they should run on the Syrtis, they lowered the gear, and
so were driven.** ¹⁸**As we were violently storm-tossed, they
began next day to throw the cargo overboard;** ¹⁹**and the third
day they cast out with their own hands the tackle of the ship.**
²⁰**And when neither sun nor stars appeared for many a day,
and no small tempest lay on us, all hope of our being saved
was at last abandoned.**

ᵇOther ancient authorities read *Clauda*

ᶜGreek *helps*

[16-20] Though driven by the sudden storm they
managed to sail **under the lee of Cauda**. With great physical
exertion Luke and others were able **to secure the boat**, in
reality a skiff or dinghy. After it was hoisted aboard the ship,
they next sought **to undergird the ship** itself. The expression
measures to undergird has been variously interpreted by
commentators and historians. One plausible explanation is
that it described horizontal reinforcement lines used to
brace or truss weak parts of the **ship**. The testimony of Pliny
would support Luke's picture. He observed in his *Natural
History* (2.48) that the greatest enemy of seamen was this
typhoon **wind**, which destroyed not only a ship's mast but
also its hull.

Syrtis was a shoal west of Cyrene. **They lowered the gear**
hoping to avert ruin upon **Syrtis**. When the violence of the
storm did not abate, **they** threw **cargo overboard** (cf. 27:38).
The following **day** they jettisoned the ship's **tackle**
(cf. Jonah 1:5).

The inclement weather stretched from **the third day** to
many days. The **tempest** was still about them; **all hope** of life
was abandoned. The worst of their crisis lay in the fact that
their navigational guides, the **sun** and **stars**, were hidden.

²¹As they had been long without food, Paul then came forward among them and said, "Men, you should have listened to me, and should not have set sail from Crete and incurred this injury and loss. ²²I now bid you take heart; for there will be no loss of life among you, but only of the ship. ²³For this very night there stood by me an angel of the God to whom I belong and whom I worship, ²⁴and he said, 'Do not be afraid, Paul; you must stand before Caesar; and lo, God has granted you all those who sail with you.' ²⁵So take heart, men, for I have faith in God that it will be exactly as I have been told. ²⁶But we shall have to run on some island."

Divine Assurance, 27:21-26

[21, 22] The physical and emotional health of this group was now in a bad way. **They had been long without food** due to sickness and not because there was no food (cf. 27:38). Paul reminded them that they had earlier disdained his advice when he was correct. This reminder by Paul was not given so much as an "I told you so," as more to compel them now to listen to his insight. Then the apostle gave a countermand, as it were, to his earlier prophecy spoken at Fair Havens. Instead of predicting the **loss of** much **life** (27:10) he now prophesied **no loss of life** (27:22). Even though **the ship** would be lost, they should yet **take heart** since no human life would be destroyed.

[23-26] Next the apostle revealed to the centurion and others that his hope rested upon a revelation of **God** himself. Specifically, a nighttime epiphany of **an angel of God** told Paul not to fear for he **must** (*dei*) still **stand before Caesar** (cf. 19:21 and notes there). Those with Paul would also be saved. Most of Paul's traveling companions (at least at this point) ignored him, probably convinced that the delirium of sickness had taken its first victim. The reader should also remember that this was to be at least the apostle's fourth shipwreck (2 Cor. 11:25, "three times I have been shipwrecked").

169

²⁷When the fourteenth night had come, as we were drifting across the sea of Adria, about midnight the sailors suspected that they were nearing land. ²⁸So they sounded and found twenty fathoms; a little farther on they sounded again and found fifteen fathoms. ²⁹And fearing that we might run on the rocks, they let out four anchors from the stern, and prayed for day to come. ³⁰And as the sailors were seeking to escape from the ship, and had lowered the boat into the sea, under pretense of laying out anchors from the bow, ³¹Paul said to the centurion and the soldiers, "Unless these men stay in the ship, you cannot be saved." ³²Then the soldiers cut away the ropes of the boat, and let it go.

Preparations for Landing, 27:27-44

[27-29] Independent estimates have shown that a voyage like that described in Acts 27:13-27 would deliver a ship from Cauda to Malta in fourteen days (James Smith, *The Voyage and Shipwreck of St. Paul*, pp. 125–128). **The sea of Adria** was that body of water which separated Italy, Sicily, and Malta on the west from Illyricum, Macedonia, Achaia, and Crete on the east. Josephus was once shipwrecked in this same sea (*Life* 3). In the dark of **midnight the sailors** heard the surf breaking upon rocks and shore. Knowing that land was nearby, they continued to sound. When they reached **fifteen fathoms, they let out four anchors from the stern**. The use of stern anchors in antiquity is well attested by other Graeco-Roman sources. These **sailors prayed**; there are few skeptics on storm-tossed ships.

[30-32] Some of **the sailors** believed their survival chances were better in a small boat which they could more easily maneuver. Under pretense of setting **out anchors from the bow,** they planned to escape by themselves. Paul's insistence that all remain **in the ship** rested upon the divine revelation. All those who stayed with Paul would be granted safety (27:24). Consequently the escape route was cut off when the soldiers **cut away the boat**.

³³ As day was about to dawn, Paul urged them all to take some food, saying, "Today is the fourteenth day that you have continued in suspense and without food, having taken nothing. ³⁴ Therefore I urge you to take some food; it will give you strength, since not a hair is to perish from the head of any of you." ³⁵ And when he had said this, he took bread, and giving thanks to God in the presence of all he broke it and began to eat. ³⁶ Then they all were encouraged and ate some food themselves. ³⁷ (We were in all two hundred and seventy-six*d* persons in the ship.) ³⁸ And when they had eaten enough, they lightened the ship, throwing out the wheat into the sea.

³⁹ Now when it was day, they did not recognize the land, but they noticed a bay with a beach, on which they planned if possible to bring the ship ashore.

d Other ancient authorities read *seventy-six* or *about seventy-six*

[33, 34] The apostle exhorted them to break their fast of a fortnight. In the relative calm **food** could be more easily eaten. Moreover, he was still emphatic that **not a hair** of their **head** would **perish** (a Jewish idiom, cf. 1 Sam. 14:45; 2 Sam. 14:11; 1 Kings 1:52; Matt. 10:30; Luke 12:7; 21:18).

[35-38] Paul broke the fast by taking **bread** and thanking **God**. This should not be taken as a record of the celebration of the Lord's Supper; breaking bread and prayer constituted the beginning of an ordinary meal by Jews. The other wearied passengers were finally **encouraged**, as Paul had been suggesting for days (27:22, 25). **Two hundred and seventy-six persons** were not too many for an Egyptian grain **ship** (27:6, 38). In *The Ship* Lucian reports the size of an Egyptian grain ship as approximately 180-by-45-by-43 feet (at its deepest). Having previously jettisoned part of the cargo and tackle, they completed the task (**lightened the ship**) by throwing the **wheat** overboard.

[39] Luke has brought the reader from night (27:27) through dawn (27:33) to **day**. **Land** was sighted, though unrecognized. And the decision was reached to take **the ship ashore**.

⁴⁰So they cast off the anchors and left them in the sea, at the same time loosening the ropes that tied the rudders; then hoisting the foresail to the wind they made for the beach. ⁴¹But striking a shoal' they ran the vessel aground; the bow stuck and remained immovable, and the stern was broken up by the surf. ⁴²The soldiers' plan was to kill the prisoners, lest any should swim away and escape; ⁴³but the centurion, wishing to save Paul, kept them from carrying out their purpose. He ordered those who could swim to throw themselves overboard first and make for the land, ⁴⁴and the rest on planks or on pieces of the ship. And so it was that all escaped to land.

'Greek *place of two seas*

---

[40] They executed three measures to facilitate landing: **they cast off the anchors**, untied the steering **rudders**, and hoisted the small **foresail**, which (as imperial coins depict) was designed to guide rather than power the ship. The plural **rudders** requires comment. Against all evidence, a few older commentaries argued that ancient ships had only one rudder. Sources from that period, including sunken ships, however, make it clear that ships had two **rudders**.

[41] The ship was grounded when it hit **a shoal**. While the **stern was** being **broken up by the surf**, the passengers moved to **the bow**.

[42-44] Soldiers were responsible for their **prisoners** (cf. Acts 12:19). The way to guarantee order **was to kill the prisoners**. This was prevented by **the centurion** into whose care Paul had been given. Those who could **swim** were ordered to jump **overboard first and make for the land**. The others were aided by **planks or pieces of the ship**. Clinging to debris had earlier saved the apostle's life, for it was probably the only way he could have survived being adrift a night and a day at sea (2 Cor. 11:25c; cf. Lucian, *Toxaris* 19-21).

All were saved by the God to whom Paul belonged and whom he worshiped (27:23) and not by sea divinities who protected sailors (see notes on Twin Brothers in Acts 28:11).

¹After we had escaped, we then learned that the island was called Malta. ²And the natives showed us unusual kindness, for they kindled a fire and welcomed us all, because it had begun to rain and was cold. ³Paul had gathered a bundle of sticks and put them on the fire, when a viper came out because of the heat and fastened on his hand. ⁴When the natives saw the creature hanging from his hand, they said to one another, "No doubt this man is a murderer. Though he has escaped from the sea, justice has not allowed him to live." ⁵He, however, shook off the creature into the fire and suffered no harm. ⁶They waited, expecting him to swell up or suddenly fall down dead; but when they had waited a long time and saw no misfortune come to him, they changed their minds and said that he was a god.

Paul on Malta, 28:1-10

[1, 2] Luke and the others learned that their refuge was the **island** of **Malta**. The ethnic and cultural roots of **Malta** were Phoenician. Even after romanization the Punic language was sometimes the local tongue. Since **natives** (*barbaroi*) did not always treat shipwrecked foreigners with hospitality, Luke mentions their **unusual kindness** (*philanthrōpia*).

[3-6] These verses reveal a facet of provincial religiosity not totally dissimilar from that evidenced at Lystra (Acts 14:8-18). **A viper** emerged from some sticks Paul had thrown **on the fire**. It **fastened** to **his hand**.

The **natives** responded to this snakebite on the basis of their pagan, animistic world view. This concept of animism believed that nothing happened on the basis of scientific law, accident, or coincidence. There was too great a sense of tragedy, they reasoned, for a person to be rescued from a shipwreck to then die at the bite of a snake. Since there must have been some special intervention by spirits or deities, the **natives** next decided that Paul was **a murderer** whom **justice** (*dikē*) sought to punish.

When even after **a long time** their expectations did not

⁷Now in the neighborhood of that place were lands
belonging to the chief man of the island, named Publius, who
received us and entertained us hospitably for three days. ⁸It
happened that the father of Publius lay sick with fever and
dysentery; and Paul visited him and prayed, and putting his
hands on him healed him.

---

come to fruition, they decided, once again on the basis of
pagan animism, that Paul must be **a god** (*theos*; see especially notes on Acts 14:11-13, 18).

Two aspects of ancient thought need to be mentioned in
order better to understand this episode. Ancient folklore
relied heavily upon the belief in a goddess named *Dikē*
(**justice**). When these **natives** of **Malta** said that **justice** (*dikē*)
smote Paul, they did not imagine our abstract concept of
justice but rather (as is clear in the Greek) the goddess
Justice (*Dikē*). Belief in the virgin goddess *Dikē* is attested
as early as Hesiod (*Works and Days* 248-73). The second
facet of antiquity behind this account is that this plot was
known in ancient literature and folklore. Two epigrams are
preserved in *The Greek Anthology* which tell of an individual who was shipwrecked, swam ashore to safety, and was
then immediately slain by an animal (7. 289, 290). In the
latter example (7. 290) the mariner was slain by a viper. He
thus received (in the thought of the epigrammatist) his fate,
from which he had only temporarily escaped when he swam
ashore.

[7, 8] It was not long until they were extended further
hospitality, **entertained three days** by a certain **Publius**.
Luke, with his typical interest in administrative titles
(e.g., proconsul, magistrate, governor, king, asiarch, centurion, politarch), reported that this man was **chief man of the
island** (*prōtos tēs nēsou*), a provincial administrative title
verified in two Graeco-Roman inscriptions. This Maltese
ruler had a **sick father** suffering from **fever and dysentery**.
Prayer and the imposition of hands led to the healing of
Publius' **father**. Whether Luke implied in this curing of **fever**

⁹And when this had taken place, the rest of the people on the island who had diseases also came and were cured. ¹⁰They presented many gifts to us;ᶠ and when we sailed, they put on board whatever we needed.

¹¹After three months we set sail in a ship which had wintered in the island, a ship of Alexandria, with the Twin Brothers as figurehead.

ᶠOr *honored us with many honors*

---

an exorcism cannot be known. No evil spirits are mentioned here, but in the Gospels, it was only Luke's report (cf. Matt. 8:14, 15; Mark 1:30, 31; Luke 4:38, 39) that contained a personal rebuke of a **fever** as though it were a demon.

[9, 10] This healing brought others to seek the same. Many **came** and **diseases were cured**. The so-called **gifts** (*timē*) may have been honors or other thanks. Some have suggested that those **cured** were treated by medical procedures (by Luke the physician) and the gifts were payment (cf. *timē* in Sirach 38:1; 1 Tim. 5:17). But if Paul received payment for divinely endowed healings, he participated in an otherwise discouraged form of thaumaturgic huckstering (see especially 2 Kings 5:23-27; Acts 8:18-24). Their thankfulness extended even to supplying their needs when they **sailed** to Italy.

Arrival in Italy, 28:11-16

[11] The normal period of wintering was **three** to four **months**. Josephus relates that **three months** were usually lost by Roman messengers winter bound in Palestine (*War* II.x.5). Pliny remarked that on February 8 the spring opened the seas to voyagers when the west wind began to soften the winter (*Natural History* 2.47). Like the ship which brought them from Myra to Malta (27:5, 6) their new **ship** was also from **Alexandria**.

Most ancient ships had figureheads representing protective deities. **The Twin Brothers** (*dioskouroi*, hence Dioscuri)

¹²**Putting in at Syracuse, we stayed there for three days.**
¹³**And from there we made a circuit and arrived at Rhegium;
and after one day a south wind sprang up, and on the second
day we came to Puteoli.** ¹⁴**There we found brethren, and were
invited to stay with them for seven days. And so we came to
Rome.**

---

were Castor and Pollux. These were divine brothers often
worshiped and prayed to by sailors. Paul knew of course
that it was the one true God who guaranteed their safety
(27:23) and that these seagoing idols were only so-called
gods and lords (1 Cor. 8:4-6). A certain Timolaus, who was
one of the figures in Lucian's *The Ship*, noted an Egyptian
ship which had been saved in a deadly storm by the **Twin
Brothers** (*The Ship* 9; cf. Epictetus, *Discourses* 2.18.29).

[12, 13] They stayed **at Syracuse**, on the eastern side of
Sicily, **for three days**, either to wait for better winds or take
aboard extra supplies for the larger number of passengers.

Arrival **at Rhegium** placed them on the Italian mainland.
Next they sailed to **Puteoli**, the port of entry for much of the
Egyptian wheat that arrived in Italy, and thus one of the
largest emporiums in Italy (Seneca, *Letters* 77; Strabo,
Geography 5.4.6; 17.1.7, who calls it by the name
Dicaearchia). Little did the throngs (as Lucian and Seneca
pictured them) at the harbor of **Puteoli** know the significance
of that day's arrival. The apostle's longing to see the
believers in Rome was on the verge of fulfillment.

[14] Since Paul **found** Christians in Italy when he
arrived, it could hardly have been Luke's purpose to show
Paul bringing the gospel to Italy (see Introduction, part 1,
pp. 14–17; cf. Rom. 15:20ff.).The **brethren** there probably
came from synagogue conversion. According to Josephus
an old Jewish community existed in this area (*War* II.vii.1;
Antiquities XVII.xii.1).

As at earlier cities so here also Luke recorded that he,
Paul, and the others were able to stay with the **brethren**, this
time **for seven days** (cf. Acts 20:6; 21:4, 7, 10; 27:3).

¹⁵**And the brethren there, when they heard of us, came as far as the Forum of Appius and Three Taverns to meet us. On seeing them Paul thanked God and took courage.** ¹⁶**And when we came into Rome, Paul was allowed to stay by himself, with the soldier that guarded him.**

¹⁷**After three days he called together the local leaders of the Jews; and when they had gathered, he said to them, "Brethren, though I had done nothing against the people or the customs of our fathers, yet I was delivered prisoner from Jerusalem into the hands of the Romans.**

---

[15] As they traveled to Rome, **brethren** from the capital city came southward along the Appian Way to greet them. The **Forum of Appius** and **Three Taverns** were forty-three and thirty-three miles, respectively, from Rome. It had been about three years since Paul wrote to the Roman Christians. Most of that time he had been in chains (Acts 21:27–28:15), but surely he recognized earlier fellow workers (Rom. 16) and precious souls such as "Prisca and Aquila who risked their necks" for his life (Rom. 16:3-5). Little wonder that he **thanked God and took courage**.

[16] The last of the "we" passages, which imply that the writer is present with Paul, occurs in the statement **we came into Rome**. The writer clearly noted that during the last two years (28:30) Paul stayed **by himself** (though able to meet with brethren like Luke, 28:30) under the guard of a **soldier**.

PAUL AT ROME, 28:17-29

Interview with Jewish Leaders, 28:17-22

[17] With determination Paul continued his quest (see notes on Acts 13:47) of the **Jews** upon his arrival in Rome. **After** only **three days** he assembled their **local leaders** (*prōtoi*, cf. 13:50; 17:4; 25:2). Once again he declared his innocence of all charges that he had acted **against the people** or patriarchal **customs** (cf. 21:21, 28; 23:29; 24:12; 25:8).

¹⁸When they had examined me, they wished to set me at liberty, because there was no reason for the death penalty in my case. ¹⁹But when the Jews objected, I was compelled to appeal to Caesar—though I had no charge to bring against my nation. ²⁰For this reason therefore I have asked to see you and speak with you, since it is because of the hope of Israel that I am bound with this chain." ²¹And they said to him, "We have received no letters from Judea about you, and none of the brethren coming here has reported or spoken any evil about you. ²²But we desire to hear from you what your views are; for with regard to this sect we know that everywhere it is spoken against."

²³When they had appointed a day for him, they came to him at his lodging in great numbers. And he expounded the matter to them from morning till evening, testifying to the kingdom of God and trying to convince them about Jesus both from the law of Moses and from the prophets.

---

[18] Paul then related that at every point the Romans had wanted to release him (23:28, 29; 25:18, 25; 26:32).

[19, 20] He stressed that he had **no charge to bring against** his **nation**, but that he had been forced **to appeal to Caesar**. His line of reasoning was to show that he was not a zealot or rabble-rouser (cf. Acts 21:38ff.) but rather a defender **of the hope of Israel** (cf. notes on 26:6, 7).

[21, 22] One does not know whether the Jewish leaders were truthful or diplomatic when they replied that they had **received** no **evil** reports about Paul **from Judea**. They desired therefore **to hear** his views **with regard to this** Jewish **sect** (see notes on 24:5). The expression **everywhere it is spoken against** reflects the growing discrimination (though not persecution) against the Christian **sect** and its militant mission.

Paul's Testimony, 28:23-29

[23] On an **appointed day** the Jews came in large **numbers** to hear Paul. For several hours the apostle expounded

²⁴And some were convinced by what he said, while others disbelieved. ²⁵So, as they disagreed among themselves, they departed, after Paul had made one statement: "The Holy Spirit was right in saying to your fathers through Isaiah the prophet:

²⁶"Go to this people, and say,
  You shall indeed hear but never understand,
  and you shall indeed see but never perceive.
²⁷For this people's heart has grown dull,
  and their ears are heavy of hearing,
  and their eyes they have closed;
  lest they should perceive with their eyes,
  and hear with their ears,
  and understand with their heart,
  and turn for me to heal them.'
²⁸Let it be known to you then that this salvation of God has been sent to the Gentiles; they will listen."ᵍ

ᵍOther ancient authorities add verse 29, *And when he had said these words, the Jews departed, holding much dispute among themselves*

---

on what he had taught an inestimable number of times in the course of his ministry, namely, **the kingdom of God** (cf. Acts 14:22; 19:8; 20:25; 28:31; Rom. 14:17; 1 Cor. 4:20; 6:9; 15:24, 50; Gal. 5:21; Col. 4:11; 1 Thess. 2:12; 2 Thess. 1:5) and **about Jesus from the law and the prophets** (Acts 26:22 and notes there).

[24-29] It was no accident that Luke with this particular scene drew the curtain on the stage of Paul's outreach to Jews. The poignancy of the situation comes both from the force of the scripture cited (Isa. 6:9,10) and the place of this scene in the structure of Acts. The reader perceives something of an almost irreversible finality in this Jewish disbelief. Just as the inception and extension of the Gentile mission were rooted in Old Testament scripture (e.g., Luke 3:6; 4:24-27; Acts 2:17; 3:25; 13:47; 15:17), so also was the continual rejection of the gospel by the Jewish nation (Luke 20:9-18; Acts 3:23; 4:25-28; 7:35-53; 13:40, 41).

179

³⁰ **And he lived there two whole years at his own expense,**ʰ **and welcomed all who came to him,** ³¹ **preaching the kingdom of God and teaching about the Lord Jesus Christ quite openly and unhindered.**

ʰOr *in his own hired dwelling*

The denunciation of Jewish obstinacy here was stronger than at Acts 13:47 (see notes there) and 18:6, as even a quick reading of these verses from Isaiah 6:9, 10 makes clear (cf. Matt. 13:14-17). What was for Paul a doctrinal truth about the recalcitrant disbelief of the Jews (cf. Rom. 9:1-5; 11:25) came to be for Luke, in retrospect, a historical truth. For with the deaths of Peter, Paul, and James (the brother of the Lord) and the destruction of Jerusalem—all within less than a decade—the widening stream which separated the church and the synagogue turned into an impassable gulf. History, moreover, gives unassailable testimony to the apostle's assertion that **the Gentiles will listen** to the preaching of **salvation** (cf. Luke 24:47).

CONCLUSION, 28:30, 31

[30, 31] With these verses Luke brings to a conclusion his two-volume work Luke-Acts, the longest contribution to the New Testament. Since Paul's life and ministry were the instruments rather than the object of Luke's theme (see Introduction, part 1, pp. 13–14), it does not alarm the reader for Luke to end without an account of the apostle's trial, journey to Spain (Rom. 15:24), and subsequent death.

That the gospel of **the kingdom** and **the Lord Jesus Christ** could have been preached **two whole years openly and unhindered** in Rome gave singular and irrefutable proof of its legality before Roman law.